DEAR YOUNGER SELF

My Advice to You

By Chris Cebollero & Friends

Dear Younger Self: My Advice to You

By Chris Cebollero & Friends

Copyright © 2019

All rights reserved. No part of this publication may be reproduced, stored in a retrieval system or transmitted in any form or in any means – by electronic, mechanical, photocopying or otherwise – without prior written permission, except as permitted by U.S. copyright law

ISBN: 9781082723247

Acknowledgements

When you set off to create excellence you often run into a ton of great folks that become part of your network. The individuals that have taken the time to join me in this project are some of the best professionals I know today. To them, I want to say thank you for taking time out of your busy schedules to share your best advice you'd share with your younger self.

A special thanks goes out to family, friends, and peers that gave their advice for Chapter 15.

Finally, to my editor. She did not want to be acknowledged, thanked, or receive any compensation. She is humble that way, and this is her personality. Well, I have a personality too, and with that said, I want to thank my editor, Debbie Stone, for her dedication in keeping me on task, her countless hours of editing, which occurred even on her vacation, and commitment to making this an exceptional project. Cheers Deb!

Table of Contents

Introduction 6

Chapter One
Stop Letting Your Emotions Control You
Chris Cebollero 9

Chapter Two
You Won't Believe What We're Going to Do!
Danny Creed 17

Chapter Three
Your Story Matters
Tricia Brouk 27

Chapter Four
Speaking Can Be Your *SUPER POWER*
Fred Miller 37

Chapter Five
Goal Setting: The Key to Sustained Success
Denise Dudley 53

Chapter Six
'Know What You Know to Be A Leader'
Lynn Scheuell 67

Chapter Seven
Asking for Help Reveals Strength, Not Weakness
Anna Smith 77

Chapter Eight
Question Authority More
Rob Wilson 91

Chapter Nine
Knowledge Unutilized is the Equivalent of Ignorance
Marcus Aurelius Anderson 111

Chapter Ten
Build Your Legacy
Rocky Ronamella 125

Chapter Eleven
When You Change the Way You Look at Things,
the Things You Look at change
Deborah L. Knight 143

Chapter Twelve
Barriers Become Speed Bumps When you are Unwilling to
Communicate, Collaborate, and Compromise
Macara Trusty 153

Chapter Thirteen
Dreams, Gone by The Wayside
Debbie Stone 161

Chapter Fourteen
Stay Connected to Your Why & Find Your Brave
Jennifer Cordia's Advice 169

Chapter Fifteen
My Family, Friends and Peers Advice to You 181

Introduction

If I could just go back in time things would be different. How many times have you heard that? Or another question, if you could, what year would you go back to and do it all over again? Just thinking about the possibilities makes me sigh out loud. Life is full of adventure, that's for sure. From missteps, mistakes, failures, and lessons learned, it created our foundations

Life certainly has a way of kicking you in the privates and then it seems to mock you as you double over in pain while you drool all over your shirt. Well, it is this swift kick into the babymaker that usually causes tons of hours of reflection, maybe a few tears, and some frustration. One thing that we have to agree on is that these were valuable lessons that made us into who we are today.

As a coach and leadership specialist, it is my responsibility to assist professionals get from where they are today and on the way to their successes of tomorrow. When thinking about writing this book, I was trying to decide what lessons I would teach my 25-year-old self. In developing this outline, a sudden realization came to me regarding experience. Over the course of the last few years, I have developed a network of amazing leaders, coaches, and professional that have taught me some amazing lessons in each interaction with them. It then gave me the bright idea to invite them to assist in the development of this project.

The individuals that authored chapters are the very best I know in their respected fields. They are committed to excellence, dedicated to development of others, and are always there when I need guidance and mentorship. I call them peers, they are mentors, but more importantly, I call them friends.

So, setting the stage, we have developed a time machine and we will be going back in time. Our mission is to impart just one piece of the best advice we have learned. That one piece of advice that, if we had known back then, would have made the journey better than that kick in the babymaker. When we stand in front of our younger selves what are we saying? What are we sharing? What advice, if we had known, would have made us better in our earlier years?

Well, since we do not have to ability to go back in time, the amazing professionals that have written these pearls of wisdom, are looking to impart their wisdom to you. To share their mistakes, successes, failures and lessons learned for your ascent towards your professional greatness.

It is all of our hope to assist you, our next generation (even the older who want and to start a second chapter in their later years), to learn from the established wisdom of these successful professionals. These experts have traveled through the muck and mire. They have already overcome the challenges and obstacles from their yesterdays, so you can side-step the same challenges and avoid what they didn't. Please enjoy their insight and practice their guidance from this day forward.

CHRIS CEBOLLERO

Chris Cebollero is an EMS Leader and Internationally Recognized Leadership Specialist, Best Selling Author, Coach and Motivational Lecturer. His dynamic and energetic speaking style has entertained, motivated and educated individuals, groups and teams for over 25 years. Chris is currently the Senior Partner of his own consulting firm specializing in Leadership Development, Individual and Executive Coaching, and Organizational Process Improvement. Chris has been seen on ABC, NBC, CBS, and FOX. He is a Certified Member of the John Maxwell Team and is an Official Member of the Forbes Coaches Council. Chris has spent 30 years in the Emergency Medical Services career field and continues to be an advocate for delivering the best care possible.

CHAPTER ONE

"STOP LETTING YOUR EMOTIONS CONTROL YOU"

ADVICE BY CHRIS CEBOLLERO

In 1990 I was 25 years old. I was a member of the U.S. Air Force stationed in Sacramento California. I was married, my son Zachery was 1, and I was both an awful husband, and dreadful parent. I was very self-centered, and thought I was more important than I actually was. My wife would soon leave me and take my little guy halfway across the country. This was the most devastating time in my life and experiencing the emotions of this separation was awful.

Some background on me, I grew up in New York City and my life was good, fun, and full of mischief. I was one of those second part of life babies, with my parents being in their low 40's when I was born. I had a brother who was 13 years older than me, and a sister that was 18 years older than me, and I was spoiled rotten. OMG, I got whatever I wanted and learned to take advantage of my newly found celebrity status. That was until my younger brother showed up 2 years later, then he became the A list celebrity and I was demoted to doing stand-ins on B list sets. I am not sure why I am using movie references, but, quite on the set.

My parents were separated and had already given their best years parenting to my siblings before I surprised them both. From this experience all I knew was when I got married, and I had my own children, I was going to do a way better job than what I thought my parents did for me. Well, so much for hope because that did not work out as planned, in fact I may have been worse to my wife and son than the effort my parents gave towards me.

Now, it sounds like my life was horrible as a boy, it wasn't. I just did not receive a lot of guidance or life lessons, but there was a ton of love, laughing, and Italian food. So, when my wife left and took my baby boy away, I deemed myself a failure and went on a self-destructive journey that would last me close to a decade.

From my intense military training, they assisted me in developing an ego the size of the state of Texas. At 25 years old I was very self-centered, extremely egotistical, and did not take advice from anyone. Going back in time before giving my 25-year-old self the advice I had to impart, and just for good measure, I would probably kick my own ass first for the foolhardiness I was displaying.

There were lots of things that led to my ego and in believing that I thought I was more important than I actually was. Regardless of how I got there, my ego was leading the way, I thought I knew better. I was the authority. I was courageous, fearless, and thinking back now, it was ridiculous and surprising I had anyone in my life to call a friend. Make no mistakes about it, my ego was one of my greatest enemies, it did not allow me to see what was right, when I was wrong, and it kept me from saying I'm sorry when I needed too. My ego impeded my ability to learn, develop skills, and it set the stage for all my early failures. When I had those failures or made mistakes, I did the only thing that was healing, I just blamed others.

So, I was allowing my ego to make all my decisions and dictate my actions. If I could go back in time and see that 25-year-old character, the advice I would give him would be to learn how to handle your ego and to control your emotions. Back then if I were able to understand the elements of Emotional Intelligence (EQ), it would have opened the door allowing me to understand who I was, how to control my temper, recognize how to motivate myself, and the empathy needed to feel emotions with others. If I were able to understand the components of EQ, it would have given me the intelligence to know that I was not as important as I thought I was.

What is Emotional Intelligence? (EQ)

In my book Ultimate Leadership 10 Rules for Success, these were the 10 rules I needed to develop to become a successful leader. Rule number one is, "never allow your emotions to dictate your actions." Learning this rule was a hard lesson and caused me to fail at everything my emotional self-set off to experience.

EQ is defined as the ability to recognize, understand, and to manage not only your emotions but to also recognize, understand and influence the emotions of those around you.

It is no secret that emotions drive our behavior and have a big impact on people. By learning the elements of EQ and how to use them in your life, this will greatly give you the leg up in every situation or circumstance you encounter.

Before we get into the elements of EQ. I want to share something that most people are amazed about when they hear it. In the 1990's American Psychologist Paul Ekman defined that there were just 5 core emotions.

- Anger
- Disgust
- Fear
- Happiness
- Sadness

I know it is hard to believe that there are only 5 core emotions. Of course, on the spectrum you can be perturbed at the low end, and on the other end be totally enraged.

One of the most vital responsibilities you can have when developing your EQ skills is to always be aware of your feelings.

It's this ability to notice your feelings, your physical sensations, your reactions, your habits, your behaviors, and your thoughts that encompass the first step in managing all of these things that may be consuming you presently. When you have the ability to be aware of all these different aspects of yourself, you will then understand what it is that other people see when they are observing you.

Another way to think of it is paying attention to your emotions or let's even call it your intuition, also known as your 6th sense or your gut feeling, that will now give you the super power to learn what, I feel, is the most important leadership characteristic you can have, self-awareness.

The Components of EQ

EQ has 5 elements that focus on your awareness, control, self-motivation, empathy and the skills you need to develop peers and relationships.

Self-Awareness

When talking about EQ, I always start off with self-awareness because I feel it is the most important component of who you are as a leader, peer, friend, and heck let's just say, who you are as a person. Self-awareness allows you the ability to have a clear perception of your personality. Your personality which includes your strengths, weaknesses, thoughts, beliefs, motivations, and, of course, your emotions. Once you have the ability to understand your own self-awareness, you now have the ability to have a bit of insight into and to understand how other people see you, understand you, appreciate your approach, and your responses to them in that particular moment. I cannot count the number of times in my life where I meant one thing and the person, I was talking to took my intention a totally different way. When you have a command of your self-awareness, it is the secret sauce to a solid foundation to your communication abilities.

As you read this section, you may have come to a quick assertion *that you are already self-aware*, and I am preaching to the choir. Well, my 25-year-old self, don't be so quick to assume. It may be helpful to have a relative scale for this awareness because you are never really at the pinnacle of understanding yourself, your emotions, or your behavior. This is a lifelong journey and really one you don't want to ever complete. Keep learning who you are, why you are, and your life will have great meaning with a solid gratification for liking you.

Self-Regulation

This is also known as self-control. I was known as a hot head. One that would respond to emotion with anger, temper, and aggression. Now that we understand how to be 'self-aware', it is now important to use that awareness to be able to have a strong 'self-control'. Daniel Goldman is an internationally known psychologist who states that, self-regulation is a star leaders' secret weapon. First, I want to talk a bit about why we get emotional. Everything we see, touch, smell, hear, and taste are all the result of electrical impulses. These impulses are interpreted by the brain and we get the end result. As these signals travel through the brain the signal passes through the limbic system, then it goes on to the frontal lobe where reasoning and logic takes place. Well, it is the limbic system that handles our self-preservation, this is where our *fight or flight* response lives. So, whatever it is we feel, if something we see makes us angry, fearful, happy, it happens in the limbic system first. So, we feel the emotion first, then the signal goes to the frontal lobe where we make logic of the feeling. Even though the frontal lobe now make logic of what we feel, it does not control the feeling. We will still feel angry, sad, etc. but this is where we are able to make sense of that feeling and decide not to react on that feeling. You may have heard it before; this is where the *think before you act* expression comes from. Once you have mastered this pause in reaction to your emotions you begin connecting your self-awareness and self-regulation connect in developing your EQ.

Empathy

Some will say that empathy is the cornerstone of EQ. Those that are students of EQ, this is their favorite component. When it comes to developing empathy, this *put yourself in their sho*e approach gives you the opportunity to see, hear, and feel things from another person's point of view. When you improve your empathy skills you will be able to build stronger more meaningful relationships. Daniel Goldman shares with us that there are three types of empathy: emotional, compassionate, and cognitive.

Emotional empathy

This is where you connect with the other persons emotions as if they were contagious.

Compassionate Empathy

This is where you have the opportunity to understand a person's dilemma, but it also allows you the opportunity to understand their feelings or emotions surrounding that dilemma.

Cognitive Empathy

This type of empathy gives you the foresight as to what a person feels or may be thinking about a situation. This is really being able to understand someone on an intellectual plane. This type of empathy is where a true connection comes from, and when you truly know your people around you, this is the ultimate expression of empathy.

Motivation

Motivation is a key component to EQ. When I teach emotional intelligence and get to motivation, people always first believe that this is the ability to motivate others. In fact, this is *your* self-motivation and self-motivation is the toughest component of becoming the best *you* that you can become. It is our self-motivation that empowers our personal and professional drive, the ability to improve oneself, this is where we develop the commitment to our goals and take advantage of opportunities. Another big part of self-motivation is how persistent we are to overcome the obstacle to reach our goals. This is where we keep optimism and the fuel that keeps our fire to achieve burning.

Social Skills

Social Skills are also called "soft skills". When you are developing into the best person or professional you choose to be, no skills are "soft" they are all tools that you need to have to ensure your ultimate success. When you have strong social skills, this allows you the opportunity to guide people in the desired direction. This is where you will need to develop your self-confidence/assertiveness, your communication, and conflict resolution skills, and how well you are able to interact with others. When you develop a high degree of social skills you are able to listen and speak effectively, you can employ your problem-solving skills, and be seen as a go too resource to those around you. You will be known for your creativity, cooperation, self-management, and ability to develop rapport over vast personalities.

When it comes to EQ, it took me too many years to find my footing in understanding who I was, and why I did things. The embarrassment of allowing my emotions to dictate my actions. When obstacles, and hurdles popped up, my response was to just quit. I lacked empathy and had no desire to develop or sustain relationships.

So, my 25-year-old self, my advice to you is to learn, practice and master the components of EQ. If you have the chance to put this skill into your personal and professional development toolbox, then most certainly you will find that success will come sooner.

DANNY CREED

Danny Creed is a Master Business Coach for success driven individuals, Executives, Business Owners, Entrepreneurs & Sales Professionals. I also deliver keynote and workshop speaking presentations to audiences worldwide, at corporate events and conferences.

I prepare my clients for massive success by utilizing Straight Talk, Real World Business, Sales & Leadership Skills & Tools that eliminate barriers and accelerate growth. My business coaching process is a powerful, individualized experience for each client. Together we get results & change lives & businesses. You can reach Danny dcreed@focalpointcoaching.com, or through his website www.realworldbusinesscoach.com or follow him on LinkedIn at www.linkedin.com/company/focalpoint-business-coaching-of-arizona/

Chapter Two

"YOU WON'T BELIEVE WHAT WE'RE GOING TO DO!"

Advice by Danny Creed

I had a dream the other night.

The dream was about two people talking, one is a teenager, a long hair country boy, dressed in bib overalls and no shirt, driving a tractor, listening to A.M. radio while he's plowing a field in Kansas nearly 50 years ago. The other is a current day, mature man, a successful entrepreneur and businessman with thinning hair. Ok, no hair.

And, both people were me.

Earlier in the evening I had watched Back to The Future for the millionth time. And, just like Marty and Doc I had somehow, someway found a free ticket on the Way Back machine, transporting through time and space for the sole purpose of having a conversation with the younger version of myself. It seems that I had a burning desire to offer the younger me some hard-earned knowledge and advice. These would be life lessons that my older, more experienced self has learned over the decades and now desperately needed to share, in hopes that my younger self would slow down enough to listen and learn and in turn, make the coming years more productive and successful.

I knew what I was up against in talking with myself 50 years younger. Back then I was a young dreamer, who only knew what the world offered by reading National Geographic and Playboy. I knew there was more out there than feeding cows, I just didn't know what. I was wide eyed with a full head of steam and bound to make a lot of mistakes as I endeavored to figure things out. And I made mistakes! I made tons of mistakes. I wondered now how different things might have been if I would have been given the same advice from a mentor from the future, back then.

I'm somehow back home, having a conversation with myself. We're standing under a huge cottonwood tree that's familiar to both of us. I can see behind us the old family farmhouse and corral.

The first thing I notice is that we're still, pretty much, the same person, just older (and smarter). Other than a lack of hair and a "time adjusted" waistline, after 50 years, we both still have the eye of the tiger and fire in our belly; we have an unwavering belief in ourselves; we still share a strong work ethic and we believe in the possibilities of life.

We recognize each other but aren't quite sure how or why this is happening. I shake hands with myself and suggest that we take a seat leaning against the old cottonwood. "I'm not sure what's going on here, but what's going on here?" he says to me.

That's my cue to begin.

I tell the younger me that I have somehow traveled back in time to help him/us live a better life in the future. I say, "Get ready for the ride of your life! Because life will offer us many amazing and incredible opportunities in the years to come." I tell him that the things that we will experience are amazing beyond what he is currently capable of even understanding. There will be incredibly happy and joyous times. And, there will be overwhelmingly sad times. People we love will die and friends will betray us. In turn, I want him to know that we'll win awards. We'll be mentored by titans of business; be in the presence of movie stars, famous musicians and legendary artists. We'll write books and rub elbows with a President, Admirals and Generals, heroes and villains, and we'll even witness a tragic moment in history. We'll travel the world and speak and teach and mentor hundreds of thousands of people. We'll meet millionaires and billionaires; we'll marry the love of our life and be together forever with children and grandchildren. We will be successful.

However, the journey won't be easy. It is a constant challenge and I now realize that there probably were better, easier and faster paths to take. There were smarter options, that with the right information and knowledge would have led us to even greater success.

I tell *me* that there are many "Great Truths" that we learn along the way, and I wanted to at least share some of the most powerful ones in our time together. So, I offer these…

1. **SHUT UP and listen!** Due to advanced innovation and technology your world will quickly change and change dramatically. AM radio will be replaced with access to unlimited channels delivered by a satellite. Everyone will have computers. Everyone will have a cellular telephone. Everything will change in how we communicate. One on One communication will become a thing of the past and thus the time honored "skill" of listening will become a lost art. People will have their heads down, addicted to their communication devices, and seemingly have lost their ability of verbal communication. Most people now listen simply to find a place to talk again, versus to listen for understanding. The art and discipline of listening has become a valued asset. So, in the years to come, I tell myself, the rule is to learn to ask questions, make a statement and then SHUT UP and listen to what your companion has to say. Listening is a learned skill and when you become known as a world class listener the most amazing things begin to happen. People want to be around you. People take you in their confidence and they will tell you the most amazing things. A valued mentor will

tell us the most powerful secret that we've ever learned about success is that if you *"Shut up and listen and your prospect or client or friend or spouse will without a doubt tell you how to help them and how to sell them. You just have to listen."*

2. **Always, Always, Always Honor Your Past!** Never abandon the knowledge that you acquire from past experiences. Draw confidence from what you already know. Every experience that you've ever had, should be a learning opportunity. Every mistake you've ever made should be a lesson learned to use in the future. We've learned that many people simply tend to repeat mistakes. People will fail at something multiple times and yet learn nothing from the experience. We will learn that the only mistake one can make is the one where we didn't learn something from it. Our rule will become a four-step process. We will learn to always ask ourselves these questions:

   Step 1: WHAT happened? (honestly evaluate the situation)

   Step 2: Why did it happen? (analyze the cause)

   Step 3: How will this never happen again? (solutions)

   Step 4: Move forward again with the confidence of this new knowledge

   When we learn to analyze our mistakes and learn from them then we will save thousands of hours in the future by learning from our lessons of the past. Take every experience, good and bad and put it into your business plan for your life. Never forget the lessons learned. Never forget the consequences of your actions. Honor every part of your life to date by improving your life and the lives around you by living and teaching your life lessons.

3. **Listen to Grandpa!** One of our most emotionally challenging periods in our life will come soon, when your Grandfather passes. So, I'll plead with you to listen very closely to any words of advice he might tell you. You'll soon recognize that he

was a guru in bib overalls. He was a life coach with dirt under his fingernails and a farmer's tan. His lessons are powerful, insightful and we will remember them for a lifetime. I still use his advice today. He would say, *"the job isn't done until it's done right!"* which was a lesson in starting and completing a task no matter how menial. He would say *"If you make a mistake, make it at full speed!"* which was a lesson in effort. Never go at a task with a dismissive attitude and a mediocre effort. When you make a mistake going half speed then you deserve the consequences. But when you make a mistake going full speed, then you can at least have the satisfaction that you gave it your all. And, he would say, *"I guess it's what's under the hair that counts,"* which was his way of saying to never judge a person by what you see. Before you can judge you need to understand them, who they are, how they think and what makes them tick. It is never what you see on the outside that counts as much as what is on the inside.

4. **Do what you love! Full of bravado and untested confidence it is easy for us to think that we are Superman.** We think we're invulnerable; nothing can hurt us; nothing can stop us. We think that we'll live forever. But we'll learn the error in this thinking. The fact is that this life is very, very short and quite precious. The time for our lives simply melts away. Days turn to weeks, weeks turn to months and years, and years turn to decades in the blink of an eye. One day we're young, the next we're old. We'll soon learn how precious our trips around the sun are. So, in this fleeting moment that is life it is ultimately important for us to try to always work at what we love. I tell *me* to never allow yourself to get into some dead-end job where you hate going to work and it becomes daily drudgery. And it will happen. Always seek out the best use of our talent. Look for careers that are challenging and where hard work is appreciated and rewarded. We will eventually work for ourselves and love

it, but until that happens be careful to not become complacent in a slow growth/no growth position where we're bored and filling time and space.

5. **Protect your time!** While we're about doing what we love, we may just as well get the subject of wasted time out of the way. We will learn the great lesson of the ages that few ever think about: Time is perishable. Time is like a banana that sits on the counter too long. If you don't eat it, it will get soft and mushy and completely inedible. Time is the same way. Once you waste it you cannot retrieve that time to use it again. Once it's gone, it is gone forever, so please protect our time. We'll learn that time really is money. The major question then is that if time is money why do we waste so much of it? The secret is to not worry about managing the time that we have in a day. The secret is, that in life we'll never be able to do everything we think or want to do. You'll need to learn as soon as possible to prioritize the things that we think we need to do and then only do the things that have the highest priority and carry the greatest consequence. The German Philosopher, Goethe said it best when he said, "The things that matter most must never be at the mercy of the things that matter least." And by the way, he said that in 1780. This is not a new principle. Learn to master time now so it doesn't master you later. We'll both benefit if you start applying this lesson now.

6. **Be disciplined.** Smart people will research what a few have known for eons; Find out what works (with anything) and then do it over and over again. Please, do us a favor. When you find something that works for you in almost any endeavor, write it down, work it out; define the steps and then be disciplined and never waver in making that lesson a habit. Our favorite definition of the word DISCIPLINE is, "The ability to make yourself do what you should do, when you should do it, whether you feel like it or not." The true secret to success

we will learn is the discipline to apply what we know on a consistent and persistent basis.

7. **No one likes anyone who makes excuses!** When you make a mistake (and you will make some world class doozies), face up to it. Admit it. Take the weight no matter how tough or embarrassing it might be. But, in turn learn to look for ways to attack the issue so it never happens again and then just refocus on the task ahead and get back to attack mode. People will notice. People will trust you when you're known as a "no excuses" kind of man, and the same people will seek you out for leadership roles. People will want you on their team. Make it a habit, no matter how hard it is, step up and be accountable. Take your lumps. Learn from the experience! Keep your mouth shut, then get the job done! You're guaranteed to attract strong relationships along the way. Remember that blame is not in a winner's vocabulary.

8. **Don't complain!** No one likes a whiner. Complaining is usually just a way to get out of a tough spot. You really must have a long look into a "Truth Mirror", one that always shows you the truth and reality of any situation. Do a gut check and ask yourself, "Am I living with a SURVIVAL mentality or a THRIVING mindset. We will meet people in our journey who live their daily lives just trying to survive and simply satisfied with just "getting by". Believe me, whether you are thriving at the time or not, the thriving mindset is the fuel that long term success is driven by. A thriving mindset understands that the glass is neither half full nor half empty. It's neither, because we know that we have the power to refill it at any time. Believe in possibilities. Believe in what could be. Believe that there we will always see a bigger mountain to climb once we have summited the one we are on. You will learn that we can literally motivate ourselves to unbelievable levels of success. And, it all starts with learning to eliminate complaining from

our life. No one in our past or in our future wants to hear it. It's always best to be known as someone who tries rather than someone who complains.

9. **Always be PROACTIVE rather than REACTIVE.** Just so you know, I tell myself, we will never be afraid of risk. Successful people are known to take action versus waiting for something to happen. Understand that living a life worried about the "what if's" will get us nowhere. Instead, learn to be aware of the "what is" and base your initiative from there. Research will show that successful entrepreneurs have one primary trait in common. It has nothing to do with age, income, gender, family status, poverty, location, education or social standing. It will be found that the single trait that all successful idea achievers share is at some point they are all willing to simply "step out in faith." That is that they are the ones that will realize when it's time to stop all planning; organizing; strategizing; talking and worrying. That there is a time when we have to just say enough! It's time to take a deep breath, say a prayer and jump into the project and just see what happens.

I begin to understand just how weird it is that I'm actually speaking to my younger self, but I take the opportunity to thank him/me for listening. I tell him that he has a lot to look forward to, but I'm not going to give away any secrets to the future or disclose any plot twists. I tell him goodbye for now.

He smiles and flashes me the peace sign.

As I walk off into the gray and fuzzy edges of my dream I turn and tell him that I just want him to know that there's an exciting ride ahead of him and that there's much more to come, much more to learn and, that our goals and dreams will never become watered down. I just won't let that happen to us. I'll tell him that today our dreams are bigger and wilder and more exciting than ever before.

Heck, we're just getting started!

Tricia Brouk

Tricia Brouk is an international award winning director. She is works in theater, film and television. In addition to her work in the entertainment industry, she applies her expertise to the art of public speaking. She's the executive producer of Speakers Who dare, a TEDx producer. She choreographed Black Box on ABC, The Affair on Showtime, Rescue Me on Fox, and John Turturro's Romance and Cigarettes, where she was awarded a Golden Thumb Award from Roger Ebert. The series Sublets, won Best Comedy at the Vancouver Web-Festival. She curates and hosts the Speaker Salon in NYC, The Big Talk an award winning podcast on iTunes and directs and produces The Big Talk Over Dinner a new tv series. She was recently awarded Top Director of 2019 by the International Association of Top Professionals and her documentary Right Livelihood A Journey to Here about the Buddhist Chaplain at Riker's Island won Best Documentary Short at The Olympus Film Festival and has been submitted for an Oscar from the Academy of Motion Picture Arts and Science. www.triciabrouk.com

https://www.linkedin.com/in/triciabrouk/
https://www.facebook.com/tricia.broukd
https://www.instagram.com/tricia_brouk/
https://twitter.com/triciabrouk

Chapter Three

"Your Story Matters"

Advice by Tricia Brouk

I was born a performer. I began taking stages at the age of 7. My first stages were in Arnold, Missouri where I wore satin leotards covered in sequins and feathers. I graduated from tap shoes and recitals to concerts and unitards, while studying for my BFA in Dance at Stephens College. And then I went on to have a very successful career traveling the world with modern dance companies like Lucinda Childs touring to stages in Paris, France, with Robert Wilson at New York City's Lincoln Center stage and more. I loved being a dancer, because it required discipline, tenacity, focus, and drive. I also loved telling a story through movement. Even when I was dancing Lucinda's solo from her Dance Suite to music by Phillip Glass on stage in Vienna, I was still telling my story. If you don't know, Lucinda Childs is a post-modern choreographer who uses maps to make dances. She's from the Judson Church era of dance and the artists from that moment in time were groundbreaking. Her work is not linear, nor does it have anything to do with a narrative. It's all counts, precision and timing. And if you know the work of composer Phillip Glass, you are aware that his music is impossible to count. That all sounds very clinical, and it was, but I still made a story out of those dances. Each and every dance I danced, had intention, point of view and narrative. This was how I expressed myself as an artist for most of my life. And it was how I worked through life's ups and downs. When I was sad, dancing made me feel better. When I was in fighting with my boyfriend, I forgot why when I was on that stage.

When I felt lost in a sea of my inner thoughts like "what the hell am I doing here in New York City", dance and storytelling kept me going. As a dancer I expressed myself through movement. I told a story with my body. I didn't have to speak. I could move. There was not a consciousness around not speaking, I just didn't have to. What I have come to know now is that I knew the power in story but was unaware of the power in my own voice. The power of storytelling, using my voice to help others use theirs has become the legacy I will leave behind in this world. I have gone from silent dancer, to award winning director, writer, filmmaker, TEDx producer and speaker coach. And I choose to help others tell their story and use my voice to support them because the power of sharing a story can change the world. I'm going to share some thoughts on how you too, can have a voice and share your story, because it matters.

Jumping off a cliff

Sometimes we have to just jump. If you want your story to unfold, it starts by putting yourself out there. And that means not waiting until you are ready. Saying yes right now means allowing room for opportunity. It means giving yourself permission to try and to fail, while knowing you'll be changed afterwards having learned something new. And it also means you have the opportunity to change another person's life. Saying yes, can be terrifying, but if you say yes, you might be surprised at what is possible. The first time I realized the power of saying yes was when John Turturro asked me if I would choreograph his feature film, *Romance and Cigarettes*. Without hesitation, I said yes. I had not choreographed anything except my college comp class, but I knew I could do it. I knew I would do it. It was terrifying. I was terrified, but not uncertain. Those are two things I want to differentiate. I held fear and certainty simultaneously. So, I went home and learned the music and made the steps and choreographed my first feature film leading me to a career of directing, writing and choreographing film, television and theater. And I got to work with the great James Gandolfini, who became a dear friend, Susan Sarandon, Kate Winslet, Christopher Walken, Steve Buscemi, Bobbie Cannavale and Eddie Izzard. I could never have dreamed I would be given an opportunity like that, but by saying yes, an entire world of possibility opened up to me. And my story began to unfold.

The second time saying yes changed my life, was when motivational speaker and thought leader Petra Kolber asked me to direct her TEDx Talk. I figured it would be just like directing any other one woman show, but what I didn't know was just how amazing it would be working with her or that it would take me down the road of starting a new business of working with public speakers. Just like before, I had no experience. I was not familiar in the art of public speaking or TED, but I did know how to analyze a script and direct actors. So, I held that as my certainty and filled in the fear part by doing my research. I read Chris Anderson's book The Ultimate Guide to TED, in one sitting. I became obsessed with the art form of TED and TEDx and I watched talks that were good and bad, becoming an expert. Both times I rolled up my sleeves, did my homework, trusting that if *yes* led me to fail, I could always get back up, dust myself off and say yes to the next unknown.

When you say yes to something that you aren't fully prepared for, run, don't walk to the nearest computer. Start doing your research, your notetaking and learn fast. Be ready to deliver and deliver hard. You have one chance when you say yes to something you aren't ready for, so you must over deliver. When you do that, you are the one they call in the future fully confident in your ability.

People always talk about boundaries and how being comfortable with saying no is so important. I think saying no to an invitation to a dinner party is absolutely the right thing to do, if you are spread thin. I say no to invitations all the time because I go to bed very early during the week and I know that if I'm out late on a weekday I'm not at the level of productivity I want to be at, so I'll say no.

What I say yes to are my needs in that moment. It may sound like I'm saying no to an invitation to the theater, but I'm really saying yes to getting a good night sleep and having a highly productive next day.

You can start saying yes right now. Wake up and say, yes, I'm going to hit the gym. Say yes, to how amazing you are each day. Say yes to a project that is out of your comfort zone and blow it out of the water. Say yes to trying something new and surprise yourself at the joy you feel. Say yes to staying at home with a good book because you are that important.

Say yes to having the biggest life possible, because your happiness will create happiness in others. And when you say yes to sharing your story and being an active participant in your story, people will be attracted to you by your willingness to say yes and your ability to back it up with expertise.

The Importance of Your Point of View

Have you ever thought about why Harper Lee chooses to tell the story of To Kill A Mockingbird, through the eyes of Scout, the six-year-old daughter of Atticus Finch? For those of you who haven't read the book, it's the story of a lawyer in the south during the depression, who defends a black man against fabricated rape charges, with a trial that exposes the children to racism and stereotypes. Miss Lee made a very brilliant, Pulitzer prize winning decision to tell the story through Scout's point of view. Not only do we come to rely on her narration, but because she's wide eyed and naïve, her point of view (POV) is crucial because it heightens the impact of the social injustices she's witnessing. POV is very important.

In film, a POV shot shows what the character is looking at represented through the camera. In the Cohen Brother's film Raising Arizona, there's a great POV shot from the baby's crib looking up at Nicholas Cage. In literature, a first-person narrative is a point of view where the story is narrated by one character at a time, just like To Kill A Mockingbird. If you are an actor who grows up in a small town, you're going to approach the work with a very different point of view, that an actor who grew up New York City. All three of these points of view, whether it's of the camera, character or an actor, ultimately help do the same thing. They help tell a story as truthfully and authentically as possible. Even though you are not on set relying on a cinematographer or making a character choice based on your point of view as an actor, you are still telling a story. The story needs to come from your point of view, the way you look at the world and in your voice. When you embrace who you are you can become the narrator of your own story. Have a clear point of view on the subject or idea you are speaking about and share these ideas through your unique lenses. We need to know how you feel about what you are talking about. How it affects you. Why it's important to you. If you feel truly passionate about your ideas, so will we. It's your POV of the world that's uniquely you. And we want to hear it spoken in your own voice.

Bad Reviews

Judging other people is something we all do, it's a subtle reflex we may not even be aware, because it happens all day long. Most people have an opinion, a reaction, a judgement about the way someone speaks, dresses, behaves. And when you put yourself out there alone, vulnerable and in front of others, like an actor, or a storyteller, it's pretty likely, you're going to be judged. Or I guess you could say "reviewed" if it's by a critic for The New York Times. Even knowing there are so many critics and judges already out there, we still judge ourselves and attach all these negative feelings to who we are. And we play the same loop over and over in our heads.

I should have done fifteen more minutes on the elliptical. I'm so lazy. I shouldn't have said that, I'm so stupid. My story is unimportant. My voice is not unique. Then all these feelings of sadness, anger, disappointment show up and we get stuck. This is the kind of repetitive thought loop that will create a negative story and could also quiet your voice.

We are constantly forming opinions about ourselves, and what we are doing and how we're doing it. This goes back to getting in your own way. Judging yourself is not just a roadblock, it's a life block. It's a cycle that will go on and on, unless you come at this from a different way, for example through some serious awareness.

When you judge yourself, try becoming aware of it. Try to get mindful. There are so many awesome mindful techniques out there, but I'm going to talk about the technique called RAIN. I like using the RAIN technique because it's easy for me to remember. It's an acronym that stands for - Recognition, Acceptance, Investigation, and Non-attachment.

When you're telling your story or sharing of yourself with the world and "I sound like an idiot. They don't care what I'm saying. I'm totally boring." Stop.

Stop immediately get mindful. Let it RAIN.

R- *Recognize how you feel*. I'm feeling overwhelmed, angry, stupid and I'm judging my writing, my performance. I'm so upset right now. Notice. Then move on to A.

A -*Accept what's happening right now*. And it doesn't mean you have to like it but try to accept it. I'm not having the best conversation. I'm really uncomfortable. I didn't show up prepared. Then start digging.

I- *Investigate the moment*. Ask yourself, "why do I feel this way?" Are you trying to impress someone? Do you feel inadequate? Don't judge yourself either, just ask the question. Then move onto N.

N- *non-attachment*. And what this means is, you are not the feeling, you're just having the feeling. You are not a stupid person; you are not an angry person. You are having the feelings of stupidity and anger. Don't attach them to who you are. Because when you do, your ability to story tell and have your voice is limited.

I'm feeling this. This is happening. Why is it happening. I'm not what I'm feeling.

Recognize, Accept, Investigate and Non-attachment

It takes tons practice but if you can remember to let it RAIN when you're struggling and having overwhelming or negative feelings, hopefully you can stop judging yourself and leave that to everyone else.

Ram Dass and Getting Hit by a Bicycle

On my way to rehearsal many years ago, I was hit by a bike crossing Houston street in New York City. I was not badly injured, and neither was the biker, but I was shaken up and didn't quite know where my body was in that moment. I still went to rehearsal and told the dancers and choreographer what had happened, and that I would be taking it easy during the run through. We did the run through and afterwards, my choreographer said that my performance was magical. That I had been able to use getting hit by a bike to inform how I moved, and that transformed his choreography to a new level. From that moment on in any rehearsal, when the dancers were pushing too hard, we'd refer to the "hit by a bike" way dancing.

And that leads me to Ram Dass.

Ram Dass is an American spiritual teacher who wrote Be Here Now, in 1971. And Be Here Now has become a very famous quote. Well, what does it actually mean?

Simply put, Be Here Now means be in the moment. When I got hit by the bike, I allowed that to inform how I danced. I was in the moment. When you are in the room with people, allow where you are that exact moment on that exact day to inform your experience. This will allow your voice to be totally authentic creating deeper relationships and far more meaningful connections with people.

The other part of Be Here Now, is simply put, don't be in the past. If you try to recreate the story of how you expect things to go every time, you'll not only be perceived as inauthentic, but you'll prevent yourself from potentially having a life-changing experience.

Being present is really hard to do. Acknowledging where we are right this very moment, and not trying to recreate the past takes courage and it takes practice. But I know you can do it.

I had no idea when I was 7 years old and taking my first stage that I had a voice and a story that would have such impact on the world. By jumping off a cliff and saying *yes* in my life, it has led me here today with you. By letting the bad reviews roll off of me, over and over again, I'm able to not waste time on the unimportant stuff and focus on putting people with important messages onto big stages. By being in the moment and having 'soft hands' as my husband Joe likes to say, I am always present, which means I can hear your voice completely and help you share your story fully. We all have a powerful voice and an important story. Remembering that can get you one step closer to sharing yours and changing the world for the better. Now go jump off *your* cliff!

FRED MILLER

Fred Miller has over 2,500 Skills Endorsements for Public Speaking and Presentation Skills Excellence! I am a speaker, an international coach, an author and a LinkedIn ProFinder Speaking Coach and Keynote Speaker. The title of my first book is, "NO SWEAT Public Speaking!" Clients, Businesses, Individuals and Organizations hire me because they want to improve their Networking, Public Speaking, and Presentation Skills.

They do this because they know: "Speaking Opportunities are Business, Career, and Leadership Opportunities." They also know we perceive really great speakers to be Experts. We like to work with Experts.

I show them how to Develop, Practice, and Deliver Knock Your Socks Off Presentations! with - NO SWEAT! You can reach me at Fred@NoSweatPublicSpeaking.com or nosweatpublicspeaking.com

Chapter Four

Speaking Can Be Your *Super Power!*

Advice by Fred Miller

If I could go back in time and talk to my much younger self, I would emphasize *this* fact: "*Speaking* Opportunities are *Business, Career,* and *Leadership* Opportunities."

In a nutshell, I have built a successful career on the premise that those who *take* and *make Speaking* Opportunities will:

- *Grow* their Businesses.
- *Advance* their Careers.
- *Increase* their Leadership Roles.

No one ever questions those statements, and why would they? Speaking in front of people is one of the most fearful things in our society. If I had the opportunity to go back in time to give advice to my 25-year-old self, it would be right to the point, young Fred, Speaking Will Be Your SUPERPOWER!

For Entrepreneurs who share the opportunity to speak to civic groups, during association meetings, and really any other events, present themselves as *Experts* and trailblazers in their industry. Speaking is one of those skills that impresses people. Of course, when it is done correctly, with passion, and conviction you will increase the credibility of you, the presenter, but also their company. This allows the opportunity to lead to new business and reinforce in the clients mind they will be making a good decision in partnering with you and your company. For those that are not in the market for your products or services, your ability to inform, entertain and persuade as a speaker is a great source of referrals. Throughout my career, I cannot count the number of times, a potential client told me 'my friend heard you at the chamber and thought you could help me with polishing my public speaking and curb my fear.'

For Individuals, when given the opportunity of speaking on behalf of their company, this gives the audiences an impression of not only who the speaker may be, but also increase the reputation of the firm they work for. Individuals should consider themselves the ambassadors for those that employ them. It is this favorable impression you give that will lead to more sales opportunities, grow revenue, and reduce attrition. Regardless of the field you go into or associate with, these businesses, associations, and organizations like to hire and promote people who know how to communicate well.

Last but not least, for **Leaders** to be successful it is vital that they must be excellent communicators. In fact, they are expected to be, and may be one of the reasons you were promoted to that position in the first place. One of the things I have found in my career is that people with the skill and ability to effectively speak to others are called upon more often than others to:

- Represent their organizations at outside events.
- Speak during meetings they attend.
- Take the lead during internal gatherings. This is really an important one, because the management of that organization knows information will be presented in a professional manner that will be easily understood by all. During that talk, coworkers will be inspired and, in many cases, emulate the skills of that speaker as they become role models.

- Take the platform to promote *the organizations* 'platform.' When working inside an organization, change is inevitable, and when the message needs to be communicated to the workforce, it is the seasoned speaker that may get the nod to bring that message to the masses.

You may be thinking that you do not need to learn the skill of public speaking and delivering because that is not the role you will be in during your career. Many young people are against standing in front of people and delivering a speech. Here is the reality, presentations are delivered all the time, every day. They occur internally as morning briefings or huddles, externally when working with clients or customers, or developing stakeholders. This can be done to one or two people in attendance, or to a larger group. This type of presentation may be less formal, and just be a comfortable conversation, but make no mistakes, you are delivering a presentation.

The Big Question

So, if speaking is so important to my career success, if speaking is a superpower, why do so many people avoid this activity? The answer may not be surprising, it is the fear of speaking publicly. It is this fear, that often is listed as one of the greatest fears people have and holds many individuals back from reaching their potential. It should not shock you to know that 75% of the population, to one degree or another, has this aversion to speaking. There is even a word for it – Glossophobia. It comes from the Greek language: Glōssa – meaning tongue, Phobos – meaning fear or dread. The important thing to note is it's a word, not a disease, and it can be lessened. Studies also show the fear of speaking is an 'Equal Opportunity Fear.' It doesn't care about a person's age, education, or occupation. I've worked with doctors to lawyers to the any person who's been asked to "Stand up and give us your 'Elevator Speech' the 'Fear of Public Speaking' is pervasive. Developing the ability to present confidently in front of an audience, even if one never does will always improve their one-on-one communication skill.

Why do people have a Fear of Public Speaking?

My question to you is why not have a fear of public speaking? Without understanding the methods of how to be a good speaker, individuals always seem to battle the uncertainty that they will forget what you are supposed to say. Maybe someone will ask you a question you do not know the answer to. This is an occupational hazard to public speaking, you will get questions you don't know the answer to, and you may get sidetracked and forget what you were saying but knowing how to maneuver those speedbumps are the true secret to developing skills as a speaker. The fear of public speaking is serious, and I'm not here to share it isn't, but it is a fear worth facing and lessening, because the rewards will outweigh the pain 10-fold. I mean think about it. Most of our conversations are one-on-one. Many are on a phone where we don't even see the other person. More and more people are communicating with email and text message, as we lose the ability to communicate face to face. So, it stands to reason if we're standing before a group and confronted with many eyeballs, most people are out of their comfort zone. That's why they're *uncomfortable!*

There are also other reasons that people fear public speaking.
1. Many do not know what they are talking about, or they try to fake their way through a conversation and make things up. Never get up in from of an audience and try to present yourself as an expert on a topic if you do not know a lot about that topic. You will never know everything, but you should have enough knowledge to 'know what you don't know.'

2. Not knowing the structure of the presentation. How many times have you seen speakers go down one bunny trail on a topic, jump to another topic, then head back to a topic from where they left earlier. Sometimes they may even repeat information, while other important information gets deleted.

    The structure of a presentation is like the recipe for a great cake, your favorite cake. It calls for specific ingredients in specific amounts, at specific times, and of course the right time in the oven. Then what do you have? A great cake. Speaking is just like that and the best way to learn that structure is to:
    - Take a public speaking class.
    - Join Toastmasters.
    - Read books and view videos on the topic.
    - Hire a coach.

3. Those who do not practice have challenges as well which leads to the fear they will forget the message they wanted to share. Practice is not optional. Consider the amount of time a professional athlete actually spends playing their sport. It is infinitesimal to the time spent practicing and conditioning themselves for their ultimate success. Why would anyone think they could take the stage to speak and *'wing it?'*

    Steve Jobs was my presentation hero. If he had a new Apple product or service to introduce at a big event he would practice for *weeks!* This is a person who was the 'best of the best. 'Bands that have been together for many years will rehearse before concerts and going out on tours. In my career I have coached people for TEDx Talks where the rule of thumb for practicing is 'one hour of *preparation* for every minute of *presentation.'*

4. Maybe a past bad speaking expereince or presentation can't be forgotten or over come. It may have been something as simple as giving a book report in grade school. Then having to sit down embarrassed and frustrated while people looked, maybe even laughed at you, that caused you to develop this

fear. Now imprinted on your subconscious as negative, it is something you do not want to ever do again. When the speaking opportunities present themselves you are hiding behind a grade school expereince.

5. Sometimes, the fear of public speaking is related to those who might be in the audience. I know a financial adviser who speaks with hundreds of clients and prospects at a time with no fear. However, if his boss or fellow advisers are there, he is a basket case because he thinks they are all judging him. Even though this is a personal obstacle, it is still a real fear and one that needs to be overcome.

6. Another fear of public speaking is coupled with how many people are in the audience. Maybe you are comfortable speaking one on one, or talking to four or five is doable, but that room full of people is intimidating. Think of this analogy; you may not mind standing on a stool, a step stool may be okay also, you may be able to climb a step ladder, but climbing a 30-foot extension ladder to clean the gutters is out of the question, and is not likely to happen

7. Let's not forget the 'What if' monster. 'What if' the audience does not like me? 'What if' my presentation is not perfect? 'What if' the last speaker was really, really good and they're comparing it to mine, and I stink? What it, What if, WHAT IF!!

8. There is also the "BIG WHAT" dilemma. 'What' am I going to talk about? 'What' have they not heard before? 'What' can I present that people will like and be interested in? My answer to this fear is - **NONSENSE!** *Everyone* has knowledge and experiences others would love to hear and will benefit from. You just have to have the confidence to make it the best you can.

Let me tell you a story.

As an Instructor for Continuing Education, I had a special class assignment for my Public Speaking Course. It consisted of inner-city church ladies who had a desire to improve their presentation skills.

The format was this: I spoke the first night and gave them the Components, Parts, and Elements of a Presentation. They came back a week later and delivered their presentations. The speeches were to be about five minutes and could be on any topic they chose.

Presentation day arrived, and I was blown away! They had worked hard on their talks and the speeches were outstanding! There were several personal stories about overcoming adversity and others about hobbies and family.

One lady waited till everyone else had spoken. I motioned to her that she was next. The woman rose from her seat and started walking to the front of the room. Before reaching the spot, people had been speaking from, she stopped, turned around, and said, "I don't have anything to talk about." Then, she started walking back to her seat. I stopped her in her tracks when I exclaimed, "Wait a minute! Don't sit down!" I then asked, "Didn't I hear you telling your classmates you speak with your children every day?"

"I do," she replied.

"What do you tell them?" I asked

"I tell them to keep away from gangs, don't do drugs, work hard, and be honest," she responded.

"That's good stuff!" I said. Her classmates nodded their heads in agreement. I asked, "How many children do you have?"

"Six." was the one-word answer.

"Wow!" I exclaimed. Looking around the classroom, I could see everyone shared my surprise. I wanted to know more, so I asked, "What are those kids doing today?"

The lady paused for a moment to think about her answer. Then, she started to speak, saying. "Four are in college, and..."

"STOP!" I exclaimed while raising my hand with my palm facing her. "You have four children in college?" I asked.

"Yes, I do." was the answer.

I responded, "That's amazing! I've got a feeling there are youngsters in your neighborhood who don't go to high school! You have four children in college and told the class you don't have anything to talk about! *We've got to hear how you did that!*"

All the facial expressions and body language in class showed agreement with my statements. The problem the lady had was she was 'too close to herself.' She literally 'didn't know what she knew."

Isn't that a great story? It's incredible, true, and it happens all the time! People think they have nothing to talk about, and their life is full of great stories to share and entertain.

To recap: One of the fears of public speaking listed above is thinking we have nothing to talk about that the audience will find interesting. The story of the lady with four children in college debunks that fear. It's a true story I love to repeat.

The big question is, what points do *you* want to make and what personal stories will you use to reinforce them?

The Imposter Syndrome.

Imagine this: You're asked to deliver a presentation to an audience of your subordinates, peers, and bosses. Great "Speaking Opportunity!" Correct?

Absolutely! However, there could be challenges. What if:
- Many in the audience have more years of service with the company.
- Quite a few have more years in the industry.
- A lot of folks are older than you?
- You perceive most attendees know more about the topic than you do?
- You believe every word you speak will be being scrutinized for its authenticity and relevance?

Thoughts like those *increase* the Fear of Public Speaking and *decrease* the quality of your delivery.

If that's your "head trash" you might have a case of *Imposter Syndrome*. Looking on the web you will see imposter syndrome defines, as a concept describing high-achieving individuals who are marked by an inability to internalize their accomplishments and a persistent fear of being exposed as a "fraud." No one I know would ever want that label.

You might also be experiencing negative self-talk as well. Some of those examples include:
- "What if they find out the truth about me?"
- "Who knows the truth and who have they told?"
- "Is there any way to stop people from finding out?"
- "Many can do this better than I can, and they should be giving this talk."

Some of that imposter syndrome comes from the fact that most of us don't like hearing people brag about themselves and are reluctant to toot our own horn. Perhaps, you are the first of your family or friends who have been in a leadership position and you're "feeling guilty" about it. If so, *Get over it!*

You were given that "Speaking Opportunity" because someone decided *you* were the best person to do that task.

Fear of Public Speaking Equals the Fear of Failure.

Actually, failing is a great way to learn. In fact, if you get it right the *first* time, you probably won't give it a *second* thought. Often when we fail, the scenario often plays out like this:
- We always seem to get upset.
- Then we try to calm down.
- We try to reflect and figure out what went wrong.
- Then we try to fix it!

That is how great learning takes place! We all do it, we all have made mistakes and have failed at something along the way. The question is how are you going to deal with it and bounce back?

Sometimes failing can be easy.
- If I'm working alone on a software tutorial, no one knows, but me, if it took thirty minutes to learn the application or three hours. Maybe, I had to watch the process a couple times, maybe I felt a bit dumb in the process. Since it was just me sitting there, is it that big of a deal?
- If I work in a closed room on a Rubik's Cube puzzle, and never complete it, I'm the only one who knows, unless I tell someone, about my 'failure.' But I won't share this failure with anyone, and hence this failure was easy. On the other hand, there are some failings that can rock you to your core and can be tough, *really* tough.

- Learning the art of public speaking can be tough. Due to the fact we are in "public" makes this a tough failure. Once we mess up, everyone in the audience knows it.
- Maybe we are giving a presentation, and the panic monster decides to drop by, and we forget what we were saying or what we were going to say next. Then we begin to panic. How would that be for a tough failure?

Don't fear my 25-year-old friend, this is why we are here, and I am excited to share with you the nuggets, the pearls of wisdom that will help you lessen the fear of public speaking.

There are a number of proven ways to lessen this fear.

1. Remember You are not alone! – There is always comfort in numbers, and as previously mentioned, many people have anxiety when they speak or begin along the public speaking route. Never use fear as an excuse to keep you from learning the skills that need to be learned. All the best speakers started with their first speech somewhere.

2. Don't admit your fear – I have heard it myself, people have said these very words, "I hate public speaking" or "I didn't even prepare for this". It is this kind of truth that will devastate a speaker's credibility. This can actually set the speaker up for failure and soon becomes a self-fulfilled prophecy. Now with this said, even though you are scared as heck inside, while you were being introduced you may not have even given the audience the impression you were afraid at all. Once you say it outload, they will be waiting for your fear to get the better of you.

3. Manage those butterflies in your stomach – You will have that weird feeling in your stomach, maybe it's a flutter, you may feel nausea. It is best to use that nervousness in your presentation. When you harness that energy, it turns a B-O-R-I-N-G presentation into a better experience. We also have to talk about the sweaty palms or shaking hands. This is a normal process, all part of your fight or flight response. Just accept it for what it is, manage the feeling in your stomach, wipe your palms, and share the information you have to give.

4. Be Audience Focused – This is why you are here. When we speak it is to inform, entertain or persuade. This is your opportunity to give them what they came for, always remember your audience when speaking. When speaking in the education arena be *student focused*, when speaking to successful companies stay customer focused, in medicine stay patient focused. This is a simple hack to becoming a great public speaker, deliver your presentations with the audience in mind, and you will see just how little anxiety you will feel. Just one more word about the audience. They want you to be successful, they came to learn something, sometimes there may be a misstep, but they will understand. Give them what they came for and give them the best you have to offer.

5. It's not about being perfect – This is one of the biggest fears, forgetting what you wanted to say, or share with your listening audience. Now, if you were an actor in a play and getting cued by another actor and you forgot you line, *you're in trouble!* When you are delivering a speech, or presentation, you are the only one who knows what is coming next. Even though you may have wanted to share something special, but you forgot, who is going to know but you? So, do your best, deliver your message, and don't worry how it comes out.

6. Meet and Greet Your Audience – This is one of the best tips I give for lessening the fear of public speaking. It is *amazing* how much easier it is to talk to people you have already met. Ensure you are the first to arrive, get set up, and them make a point to shake hands, make eye contact, and thank as many people as possible for attending.
7. Remember people's names – Everyone likes to be remembered, and sometimes this can be a daunting task. If need be, use name tags, this is an easy way to put names to faces, and easy to remember in the long run.
8. Know your stuff – Become the expert on your subject you are presenting, this will assist with building your confidence in your competence of delivering the subject matter.
9. Provide a road map – During your opening it is always best practice to share a bit about the topic you will be presenting, and in which order it will be coming. This road map will allow those listening to know what is coming next. Another big part of this is sharing how you will be handling questions during the talk. This is a biggie!

The Silver Nugget

There is one more Silver Nugget to lessen the fear of public speaking and to becoming the very best speaker you can. In Real Estate you always hear the secret to finding a great business location is Location, Location, Location. Well, there is one for becoming a great presenter as well. It is Practice, Practice, Practice. This is it, nothing scientific, or earth shattering, it is all about preparing for your talk.

This is not an optional, it is vital to the success of your presentation. There is a great quote by Malcomb Gladwell that says, "Practicing isn't the think you do once your good. It's the think you do that makes you good". A good rule of thumb I share when helping prepare TED talk Speakers is for them to prepare one hour for every minute of presentation. I know, it may seem excessive, but think about professional athletes. The amount of time actually spent playing their sport, be it football, track, baseball is infinitesimal to the time spent working out and practicing.

Ways to Practice

When practicing to deliver a speech there are many ways to practice, it may be as simple as reading over your outline, speaking to your mirror, or maybe delivering the talk to your friend, family or favorite pet. One of the things I share with my clients is to use voice or video recording to watch and listen to yourself after each practice session. This is a great way to hear your pronunciation, and enunciation of words, how your voice projects, and gives you a feel for your speed, tempo, and voice inflections.

If you are going to make a video this will give you the best opportunity to see how you will look during your talk. You can watch your movement, how you are gesturing with your hands, and how you use your body to make points.

Yes, my 25-year-old self, public speaking is a vital component of your success throughout your career. This is the one e of the best secrets I can give you for making your transition into the business world the most valuable. Learn the art and science of speaking, feel comfortable with your ability, and watch how your career blossom. Delivering a great presentation can be your superpower when you face your fear, use the above roadmap and make your presentation – **NO SWEAT!**

DENISE M. DUDLEY

Denise M. Dudley is a professional trainer and keynote speaker, author, business consultant, and founder and former CEO of SkillPath Seminars, the largest public training company in the world, which provides 18,000 seminars per year, and has trained over 12 million people in the US, Canada, South Africa, Australia, New Zealand and the UK. Denise holds a Ph.D. in behavioral psychology, a hospital administrator's license, a preceptor for administrators-in-training license, and is licensed to provide training to medical professionals in the United States and Canada. She's also a certified AIDS educator, a licensed field therapist for individuals with agoraphobia, and a regularly featured speaker on the campuses of many universities across the US, and the author of Simon and Schuster's best-selling audio series, "Making Relationships Last." Denise speaks all over the world on a variety of topics, including management and supervision skills, leadership, assertiveness, communication, personal relationships, interviewing skills, and career readiness. Denise's latest book, "Work it! Get in, Get noticed, Get promoted," is currently available on Amazon.com, and is receiving all 5-star customer reviews.

Be sure to follow Denise on LinkedIn, Facebook, Twitter, or on her website:

https://www.linkedin.com/in/denise-dudley-425a74142/

https://www.facebook.com/Denise-M-Dudley-705284789656448/

https://twitter.com/contactdenised1

http://denisemdudley.com/

Chapter Five

Goal Setting: The Key to Sustained Success!

Advice by Denise Dudley

Hello there, 25-year-old Denise! Wow. I just gotta tell ya… you're about to have the most interesting life! Too bad you don't realize it right now, but you're well on your way to some great adventures, and yes, more than a few ups and downs, but ultimately, a successful career and personal life that you will totally enjoy—and be very proud of.

Let's see here. What do I wish I could've told you, way back when? Well, there are some obvious things, like don't worry about the small stuff, wear sun screen (spoiler alert: wrinkles are headed your way!) and be sure to practice gratitude each and every day. But like I just said, those are the "duh" sorts of things you wouldn't have been surprised to hear from your older, wiser self. Digging a bit deeper, though, here's the "golden nugget" of what I want to say:

Set some clear and specific goals for yourself!

Even as a 25-year-old, goal setting would've gotten me farther down the road—and in a more organized direction—than randomly wandering about the planet in search of whatever I might have been looking for at the time. (My current self can't exactly remember what I was thinking back then!)

So, let's jump right into my chapter on goal setting.

The first thing I want to tell all you 25-year-olds (give or take a few years) who are reading this chapter is that you're going to face some hard times during your career. There may be periods when it seems like the entire world is conspiring against you, and you'll feel like running off to Tahiti to lie in the sun and eat breadfruit for the rest of your days. Unfair things will happen. At times, you may even start to lose hope. So for all those times when you find yourself at the end of your rope, here's a little hard-earned advice: Take a break if you can, try to detach from the problem and get some perspective on the matter, and realize that you won't know the outcome until time (maybe plenty of time) has passed.

Allow me to share with you one of my favorite maxims, which has proven true over and over again throughout my life: *Sometimes you can't tell the bad news from the good, especially when you're stuck in the middle of it.* So, keep your eye on your goals and don't give up on your dreams, no matter what the circumstances.

That little saying comes from direct personal experience. There've been countless times in my life when I believed a "bad thing" was happening, only to find out, perhaps several days or months later, that the *bad thing* was actually the *best thing* that could've possibly occurred—I simply didn't know it at the time.

And so, you may be going through absolute despair, the driest of dry spells, or the losing streak to end all losing streaks. Lost that job? Passed over for the promotion? Broken up with your soul mate? Been outbid on the house you had your heart set on? You truly won't know whether this "disaster" is bad or good until you've gained some time and perspective and can determine what happens *next*. Then, you just might find out it was the best thing that could have happened to you. And that's why *goal setting* is vital to your success—you'll have something positive to aim for when times become tough and you're looking to discover the silver lining among the storm clouds.

Goal Setting is the jumping-off point

In the same way that a company or a corporation needs a well-thought-out business plan that contains viable growth strategies and metrics, you and your career need a plan. If you want to learn, grow, and succeed, you will need to define your goals and develop a reasonable strategy for accomplishing them.

The continual setting and achieving of goals IS the foundation of a satisfying career—or, quite often, it's the continual setting and *modifying* of goals before they can be achieved. (And, while we're on the subject, goal setting is also the foundation of a satisfying *life*.) Of course, there are some people who have enjoyed glorious careers that seem to have dropped into their laps. We've all heard about Natalie Portman being discovered by a Revlon cosmetics agent in a pizzeria on Long Island and poof—just like that! — she became a star. Hugh Hefner's daughter, Christie, became the CEO of Playboy, Inc., and probably *not* because she worked her way up from the mailroom. And Steve Forbes, editor-in-chief of *Forbes* magazine and CEO of Forbes Publishing Company, inherited the job from his father, Malcom Forbes, who inherited it from *his* father, B. C. Forbes. Sometimes, being in the right place—or the right family—at the right time pays off.

For the rest of us, though, setting goals is absolutely crucial: In order to get somewhere, you must choose a direction. And then you must start moving toward it. (Several years ago, I wrote one of SkillPath Seminars' registered tag-lines: "Pick a Direction and Grow." That's how much I believe in goal setting—enough to put it on the cover of our company catalogs.)

But not just any old goal will do. Certain goals can sap your confidence, make you feel like a failure, and carry you off in the wrong direction. Still others can leave you spinning your wheels, getting nowhere. But some goals—the right goals—will spur you on to success. Like a beacon in the night, they'll continually lead you down the right path, as long as you keep focusing on them.

So how do you set goals that help rather than hinder? There are five essential parts to a worthy goal. It should be:

Reasonable:

"One day you can be president of the United States if you really want to," they told us when we were kids. And they insisted we should always "aim for the stars." Sky-high career goals may be inspiring for some, but they can be self-defeating for the majority of people. (Let's face it: Only one person at a time gets to be president, which leaves the rest of us out of a job!) That's because impossible or nearly impossible goals practically ensure you'll feel like a failure if or when you don't achieve them. And when that happens, you may just want to pick up your ball and go home. To avoid the "impossible goal syndrome," break down your long-term goals (e.g., getting into management) into something more realistic. Set smaller, bite-sized, daily goals, like showing up for work on time, spending at least 15 minutes networking with people who can help you, and getting all the way through a reasonable to-do list. These repeated successes will build your feelings of personal fulfillment *and* your confidence, while steadily moving you closer to your larger, long-term goals.

Specific:

Set clear-cut, simple goals. Instead of saying something vague like, "I want to move up the career ladder," say, "I'll get a degree in my field," or "I'll make sure that all my reports are on time and accurate." Once you've pinpointed some goals (no more than five at a time), write them down and say them out loud. Committing them to paper will make them more concrete. By thinking about them, saying them out loud, *and* writing them down, your brain will build multiple strong connections to your goals, making you more likely to be successful!

Measurable:

This goes hand in hand with being specific. Make sure your goals have clear outcomes that you can see or quantify in some way. Instead of saying, "I'm going to be a better employee," say, "I will contribute at least one constructive idea at every staff meeting." This will make it easier for you to track your results. Either you reached your goal, or you didn't.

Adjustable:

If your goal is too rigid or impractical, it might not be attainable. For example, let's say you've set a goal of getting your master's degree no later than one year from today. But if you are working full-time, have two small children, and have suddenly found out you must vacate your apartment and move across town, your timeline for getting that degree will probably need to be lengthened. Or you may decide that it isn't really necessary, or maybe it's not something you truly want to do. Goals require not only ability and drive, but commitment and opportunity. Reevaluate each goal periodically and decide if it's still something you really want to pursue. Then give yourself the opportunity to change your mind or create more realistic or desirable goals. (Case in point: About 10 years ago, I changed my mind about wanting to learn to skydive. Jumping out of an airplane and hoping the parachute opens? What was I *thinking?* Sorry, avid skydivers—maybe I'm just a chicken!)

Given a time frame:

Setting a deadline is particularly important, especially if you tend to procrastinate. Without a deadline, it may be hard to find a reason to act *right now*; there's no real sense of urgency. So, pick an end date for achieving your goal (again, write it down), as in, "I'm going to make 10 cold calls before noon every day for one month." On the end date, evaluate. Did you reach your goal? If so, pat yourself on the back. If not, ask yourself if you may have set your goal too high. Was it too complicated? Did you work hard enough at it? Was it something you really wanted to achieve? You may find that your goal needs to be tweaked, changed, or even possibly abandoned.

Make sure all of your career goals are reasonable, specific, measurable, adjustable, and given a time frame. And when they seem obsolete or they no longer work for you, get rid of them and set new ones!

"Got it, Denise. I hear you and I'm working on it…"

Okay, let's say you've set your goals, and you're doing your best to find your dream job (or at least a close proximity), but you haven't yet found what you're looking for. In fact, maybe you're far from it. You may be a gofer for some autocrat or sitting in a windowless room inputting reams of data in a huge IT department, or literally scrubbing floors. Well, here's a little secret: Whatever it is you're doing, no matter how insignificant it may seem, if you do it with excellence, you'll be noticed. And you may even be promoted. If you want to stand out from the crowd, move ahead, and achieve your goals, no matter what your current position, do the following:

Be the best at something.

Because it's so unusual to see a person who *really* excels at his or her job, someone in the higher echelons is inevitably going to think, "Hmmm, I wonder whether we should consider them for another position …" That's why you should set your sights on being the very *best* sandwich maker, floor scrubber, or assistant-to-the-assistant you can possibly be. It may not be a glamorous job right now, but if you demonstrate excellence, it's highly likely that you'll move up—and probably sooner rather than later.

Meet your responsibilities.

One of my mentors once told me, "Just show up on time and do your job, and you'll be ahead of 90 percent of the other people." And, in the working world, I'm afraid it's all too true. However, this makes it that much easier for *you* to look great.

So be punctual, always. Take your job responsibilities seriously. And see to it that your work is completed properly and on time. It's amazing what a good impression you'll make simply by doing what you're supposed to do.

Do more than you're asked—and do so cheerfully.

When Rachael Ray was in her early twenties and selling fancy foods at a gourmet food shop in Albany, New York, she noticed that her well-to-do customers bought prepared foods but shunned the grocery aisles. That's because they either didn't know how to cook or didn't want to spend the time. So, Rachael started doing in-store demonstrations, showing her customers how to make quick, delicious, no-fuss meals. Her demonstrations became wildly popular and sold out quickly, and it wasn't long before a local TV station asked Rachael to do a regular segment featuring her "30-minute meals." Her career as a TV food star was on its way.

Rachael's demonstrations were her own idea, the result of her boundless energy and enthusiasm. And you can do the same. Look around your workplace and see what needs to be done. Is there a problem you might be able to solve? A mess you can clean up? A way you can improve things, not only for yourself, but also for others? Do *more*— it's a great way to get noticed.

Say "yes" to things nobody else wants to do.

I may have a PhD in psychology, but I began my career on the very bottom rung—as an aide in a psychiatric hospital. Almost immediately, I became a psychiatric assistant, but my job duties were far from glamorous: I got the patients up and dressed, fed them, took their vital signs, broke up altercations (they often hit each other, and us, the staff), supervised smoke breaks (which meant I had to light everyone's cigarettes and make sure they didn't smoke them down to their fingers—and I truly hate cigarette smoke!), and many other similar chores. I also had to clean up lots of messes of all kinds. (Go ahead and let your mind wander—you know what I'm talking about!)

Early on, I vowed to stay pleasant, no matter what, and often volunteered to take on patients who were combative and difficult. It was rough, tough, physical work, but I loved the patients and they loved me back. One day, there was a particularly bad smell coming out of a locked closet assigned to a patient I'll call Alice. She was difficult, violent, and almost impossible to handle, but she liked me, so I volunteered to go into her closet and find out what was going on. There was just one big problem. Alice could become extremely agitated and aggressive if anyone touched her body or her possessions.

As gently as possible, I tried to explain to her that something in the closet had gone bad and we needed to find out what it was and get rid of it. Alice protested and cried, but finally relented; then a few of us donned gowns, masks, and gloves and approached her closet. I unlocked the door and made a gruesome discovery—stacks and stacks of used sanitary napkins. Alice didn't want to throw them away because, as she described it, they were "part of her body." I pulled the ghastly mess out by myself, piece by piece, and the other staff members carted it away.

Yeah, it was pretty gross. But I did it anyway, with as much professionalism, positivity, and empathy for Alice as I could muster. And I believe my willingness to tackle all kinds of chores like that one helped to make me a standout—showing that I was a team player, a hard worker, and the kind of person who could handle just about anything. It was undoubtedly a major reason that I moved up fast in that organization, becoming corporate clinical director while still in my twenties.

Countless people have climbed the career ladder this way—by taking on clients no one else wanted to deal with, doing dirty jobs, staying late, and working on holidays when everyone else was off having a good time. It might be unpleasant or even difficult, but it can solidify your image as a go-to person—one who can accomplish the impossible and work with the unmanageable.

Take chances.

Once you've chosen a direction, you'll encounter many forks in the road—times when you can either play it safe or go out on a limb. In most cases, I think it's best to go out on a limb; that's where you're more apt to reap the benefits. For example, when an enticing job opportunity arises, go for it—especially while you're young. Hanging on to your current job because it's safe and provides a regular paycheck can lead to years (or an entire career) spent stuck in the same position. In large corporations, there's an adage that often holds true: To reach a higher position, you sometimes have to go away and then get hired back. This means that the longer you sit in your current job, the more likely you'll be viewed as a person who can handle only that position. In short, if opportunity beckons and it looks reasonable, take a chance! Almost everyone who has ever moved up the career ladder has taken a gamble like this while reaching for the stars.

Next, let's add a little oomph to our goal-setting formula: positivity and passion!

Here's something I discovered over the years: Successfully achieving your goals is almost always the result of two things—*positive thinking*, the belief that you can and will achieve your goals, and *passion*, the energy, enthusiasm, and drive you need to get to the finish line. If either is in short supply, reaching your goals will be a whole lot harder, if not impossible. Nothing can derail you faster than doubting yourself, waffling, or beating yourself up for things you've done wrong. And if your passion wanes (or, God forbid, runs dry), facing and overcoming the challenges you'll encounter can become overwhelming.

So, here's my advice: Muster as much positive energy and passion about your goals (and *yourself*) as you possibly can, because you're going to need it! And I'll take it one step further: Become positive and passionate about *everything you do in life*. The rewards you reap will be endless. I know this empirically, because positive thinking and passion have played crucial roles in every single one of my achievements, and I'm sure they will for you, as well.

And guess what? No matter what you may be doing, you *can* develop positivity and passion for your life as it stands right now.

I know what you may be thinking. "This woman is nutzoid-crazy—I'm working as a dishwasher on the midnight shift at the Greasy Spoon!" However, you're just going to have to believe me on this one. Your day-to-day job may be less than thrilling, but if you make a conscious effort to become positive and passionate about it and perform to the best of your ability, it will have amazing effects on the way you feel and are seen by others. Your energy levels will increase, you'll accomplish more, you'll enjoy your job more, and you may even be considered for a promotion.

Becoming passionate about your life in the present tense is the first step toward moving ahead and achieving your goals!

I once knew a security guard named Martin whose main job was to direct traffic in the parking garage of a large corporation where I was doing some consulting work. Martin threw himself wholeheartedly into this seemingly boring position, enthusiastically waving "good morning" and "good night" to every person who drove by, directing traffic with energy and attention to detail, high-fiving other employees as they walked to their offices, and generally reveling in being the star of his own show. He was a blast to watch in action, and I always looked forward to his enthusiastic "hellos" whenever I'd arrive at work. Soon everyone knew Martin's name and spoke fondly of him. And it wasn't long before Martin was promoted to manager of the security department.

Do you suppose Martin's sole career goal was to be a security guard? Do you think Martin was truly excited about directing traffic when he was given that assignment? My guess is that he was not. But he became positive and passionate, and in so doing, he thrived, was promoted, and achieved one of his lifelong goals of working in a management position.

Increasing the passion factor

How can you become more passionate about what you're doing right now, even if it's not your favorite thing? Try the following:

Throw yourself enthusiastically into your duties.

It's so true that the more you put into something, the more you'll get out of it. Don't hold back. Channel Martin!

Act as if you already love what you're doing.

This is one of those "fake it 'til you make it" things, and it totally works. It really *will* help you muster true passion, because of an interesting and useful behavioral fact: Behavior *always* precedes emotions and feelings. In other words, *act* as if you are passionate, and you will eventually *feel* passionate.

Find creative ways to accomplish routine tasks.

Put your own unique spin on your job, as long as it's within the realm of what's considered acceptable at your workplace. You'll be more energized, and maybe even entertained.

Look for learning opportunities so you can keep growing.

The more you learn and grow, the more interesting your job (and you) will become. Beware of stagnation; it's a passion killer.

Create a positive aura around yourself.

Make sure you think positively, put out only positive energy, and surround yourself with positive people. Negative thoughts, energy, and people will drain you and hold you back. (And while you're thinking about this, give your personal life a good look-over, as well. Negativity is crippling and debilitating wherever you encounter it, including in your relationships with acquaintances, friends, and family members. You may need to 'clean house!')

Practice selflessness and give more than you get.

Perhaps it will seem counterintuitive to you, but both will invigorate you and ignite your passion. You will find almost boundless satisfaction and energy by making the world a better place through your caring and compassion.

Laugh about your troubles, whatever they may be.

Obviously, this isn't always possible, especially if you're feeling tired or frustrated. However, it may be more feasible than you might think. You may need some time and distance from problem situations before you can do this, but if you can have a good laugh at what's bothering you, it will seem less daunting. I do this as much as possible, and it works!

All of the above points will help you find and increase your positivity and passion—two things you'll need in large quantities in order to achieve your goals. Just choose one or two suggestions, put them into play, and see what happens!

And finally, just keep moving!

As Albert Einstein said, "It is the same with people as it is with riding a bike. Only when moving can one comfortably maintain one's balance." The same is true with your goals. Keep pursuing them, and then set new ones as soon as the old ones are either realized or discarded. Always do your best, take the jobs no one else wants, think of new ways to improve the current situation for yourself and others, and plow ahead. You'll get somewhere eventually, although it might not be the *exact* destination you'd originally imagined. Still, doors *will* open for you, as long as you continue to walk down that hallway toward personal success.

Good luck my 25-year-old self, you will make mistakes but with positivity and passion in your life it will be full and wonderful. Best wishes!

LYNN SCHEURELL

Lynn Scheurell is a professional catalyst, intuitive and best-selling author. As an authority on translating nebulous and/or complex concepts to clear, concise language, she effectively communicates life-changing ideas with clarity.

Since 1998, she has worked with more than 10,000 people in more than a dozen countries to discover their unique essence to deliver it through their businesses, books and presentations. She teaches why you're getting the results you are getting now as well as how to manifest the results you want through intentional clarity.

By definition, a catalyst provokes significant change; this is what people expect in working with Lynn. She is an innovator and facilitator of the complex made simple. Concurrently, Lynn also knows the proven keys to business success in systems, marketing and strategic action. She has also developed her innovation and brainstorming skills, lateral systems thinking capabilities and high sensitivity to unseen energies that can be utilized to optimize flow and intentional results.

Focusing on writing several books, she currently resides in Southern California. She considers herself to be a practical visionary, idea generator and facilitator of positive transformation through clarity consciousness.

Lynn can be reached at her personal website at: LynnScheurell.com.

Twitter: Twitter.com/LynnScheurell

Facebook: Facebook.com/MyCreativeCatalyst

LinkedIn: Linkedin.com/in/lynnscheurell/

CHAPTER SIX

'KNOW WHAT YOU KNOW TO BE A LEADER'

ADVICE BY LYNN SCHEURELL

Being responsible for recruiting members for a large, newly merged association was rigorous. It was a fairly new position, having been created post-merger, so nobody really knew what it required – only that the organization needed new members to fuel on-going corporate and administrative activities. The annual dues were a percentage of the organization's operating budget. As a result of the association's human-services mission, nobody really understood sales – especially my boss. And I was a young go-getter who stirred things up in an established infrastructure that was navigating tremendous change. In other words, it was chaos without sales leadership.

Despite my youth at the time, I had always been naturally adept with sales conversations. It's like I have a homing sense that tells me exactly what needs to happen next to close on a deal. For example, this association had been formed around 1900 to serve organizations that help people and communities. There were two 'paths' to such organizations, which still formed the backbone of today's human services movement. Being naïve, I jumped in and started making calls; one of the very first calls I made was to a large organization that was the other 'half' of the movement from which this association sprang. I didn't know any better, so I asked – and got – their membership. It was a pivotal moment in healing the two branches that formed nearly a century ago during the social services movement. And it was a nice feather in my newly acquired sales hat.

While making such recruiting calls, I also spent time building a database of human services organizations. I felt it crucial that we have a target list of contacts. Now we would call this account-based marketing; back then, it was leading-edge. Since this was before the availability of online database lists, I was building this contact list by hand. I spent a lot of time on it and eventually, over three or four months, I had built it to several thousand entries (about 20% of the market). Throughout that entire time, my boss told me not to work on it; I shook her off time after time and we would 'battle' (in a way that only human services professionals can – politely and indirectly). Finally, she put her superior-ranking foot down and told me NO, that if I continued to work on it, I was risking my job. Within two months, I transferred out of that department feeling conflicted. I had been back-burnered and just KNEW we needed that list. But I re-focused my career and went on in a new direction.

Fast forward to about eight years later… I was back in town visiting and something told me to pop in and see who, if anyone, might be around to say hi. As I was rounding the corner down the hall, I literally ran into the IT administrator. I was floored to see that a) he was still there, and b) he had my big binder of contacts in his hands! When I asked about the binder, he said there was pressure to recruit new members and he had remembered my project from way back when, so he pitched it to the C-suite as a potential solution. And they loved 'his' idea! They thought it was avant-garde and worth pursuing so they put him on building out my list further. That was a moment of personal validation for me, albeit very late and serendipitous in nature.

I have always remembered the lessons gained from this one experience – to know what I know and trust it. Over time, I have come to learn that personal clarity, fueled by instincts, is a key to success on multiple levels, especially leadership.

Leaders Are Ordained

We follow those people who take us to places we could not (or would not) go on our own. A leader cannot effectively self-proclaim their leadership; instead, it is the people who form their following who ordain them as a leader.

To be a leader, one must be willing to break the status quo, to go against the grain, to challenge the obvious, to go beyond the expected, familiar and predictable. As a leader, you must honor your own instincts. It doesn't mean you can't change your mind as you get more information! Instead, you must trust yourself enough to follow through on your insights. Your clarity is what builds confidence in yourself and others. Your discernment is what inspires others and blazes new trails. And it can only happen when you believe in yourself.

However, the ability to do so is a journey. Why? Because we are conditioned to play nice, to not upset others and to conform to the judgments and standards of others. Generally speaking, society focuses on building up our limitations rather than strengthening our potential because that is less quantifiable. In school, we're taught to pull up our grades and work harder on what we score low in instead of building up our natural strengths. We're not taught to think for ourselves; instead, we're taught how to follow the rules, memorize the facts and rely on our intellect and the information we receive with our physical senses. That's not a bad thing – in fact, our schools have a tough job to do and I applaud the teachers who do it despite the circumstances they face daily.

But no school I know of teaches kids how to listen to their inner wisdom - and we pay the price as adults. We make decisions because of other people's opinions or expectations, because that seemed logical at the time, or we take the easiest way because why take the harder one? We humans tend to take the path of least resistance. It's hard to be a non-conformist, a rule-breaker, a leader.

And then we interpret the challenges that come up as a result to be a reflection of our self-worth. We believe we didn't make the right decision because we are somehow wrong in our thinking, which is usually not the case. We made the decision we did because of external influences instead of listening to what we know from the inside.

A leader cannot take the risk of playing small. A leader learns how to express their ideas in a way that compels their authority and credibility. The journey is that, over and over again, a leader in the making will typically experience a reevaluation of their self-worth based on how they are being interpreted by the world around them. People who are not strong enough to be emotionally resilient will not make it to a leadership role. But when they do, that leader has learned to trust what they know, how to overcome stagnancy and, ideally, tune into and project their charisma. They become worthy of being followed. They become ordained.

Leaders Do Not Conform

Consider business leaders who have had great impact on the world – Steve Jobs, Oprah Winfrey, Jack Ma, Bill Gates, Richard Branson, Elon Musk, Jeff Bezos… you name the leader – and you will discover someone who shook off convention to do something different.

In doing so, that leader risked judgment, failure, ridicule, money, pride… but they knew what they knew, and they followed it to completion. Completion did not mean a buttoned-up product; instead, completion meant 'good enough' to get their idea to a place where others could see it to buy into it.

No conformist ever made history. Non-conformity means going against the grain, being on the 'fringe' of conventionally accepted wisdom, being a target for people's fears and resistance to change. As a leader, you need to know what you think will not always be popular. You will pose ideas that threaten the worldview of the people around you. You will become a lightning rod for projections, problems and power moves by others who are invested in the status quo.

To the degree that you shake things up is to the degree that you have power. If what you are doing or thinking is of no consequence, people won't react. However, when you are leading a new initiative, movement or project that can disrupt the safety, security and stability of others, you will find yourself pressured in creative ways to stop what you're doing.

At the same time, people need change, variety and to progress in new ways to stay vibrant. Leaders who are willing to risk others' growing edges are those we follow to new places. The key for the leader is to know what they know.

How to Know What You Know

Leaders are compelled by a different 'hum' in their lives... they know there's something more, they want to make a bigger difference, they have a unique perspective (idea, process, etc.) they are driven to share to create value. But sometimes they don't have a grip on what it is exactly that they know.

Knowing is an elusive concept. It is ironic that 'knowing' feels so uncertain. My theory on that is we are socialized out of trusting our own knowingness and taught to depend on external credibility for a lot of things - validation, approval, permission, proof, measurement, and more. It's natural that something as intangible as 'knowingness' is difficult to pin down and call out as a certainty.

There are societies still living in remote parts of the world that rely only on knowingness to live their lives. Intuition, instinct, trust, faith and perception are the keys to their world. What would it be like if leaders could do that too, surrounded by all the other gifts of the Western world (intellect, judgment, logic, etc.) without being dominated by them?

There are a few things that can help you anchor what you know, as follows.

1) Trust you are always getting your messages, in right timing, to the degree you can interpret, take them in and do something with them. (If they're too far ahead of where you are in the moment, you won't have a frame of reference for them - but they will return when you're ready.)

2) Have faith in your power of free will to act on what you know. When you do (and you will) get unexpected results, you can always make a different choice.

3) Be responsible and accountable for what you 'know'. Just as you can't un-ring a bell, you have access to fresh information which becomes part of the fabric of your life. Denial is not really an option.

4) Let your body help by feeling your 'knowing'; give yourself the experience of understanding your physical language of knowing. (Hint: play with that by holding something in your hand and asking if it's optimal for you - if your body leans in, that's a yes.)

5) Nobody else can 'know' for you better than you can... this is all about internal authority over your domain, regardless of what you see with your eyes (circumstances, relationships, opportunities, resources, environment and more).

6) Knowing can be contrary to what you expect / want. Try not to judge the messages of insight you get; instead, note and contemplate them to see their potential in creating positive change.

7) Your 'knowing' will always add to your life experience in the long run and, generally, does not hurt anyone else. However, if your 'knowing' says it's time for a relationship to end, that may hurt as this situation gets resolved, but it's necessary for growth – and, usually, for you and the other person.

By allowing your 'knowing' to express the truth of what you know, you are stepping into a new way of leadership. While the process of trusting what you know usually contains a lot of "I don't know" (how to do it, if I can, where the resources are, etc.), that is the jumping off place for your innate knowingness to kick into gear. It's really where you want to be - the place of not knowing so you can be open to perceiving what you know at a much deeper level.

Leadership Through Wisdom

Wisdom is applied learning over time; leadership is showing up over time with vision, clarity and a voice. In both cases, there is no conclusion, no ending, no achievement – it is a continuous process of evolution. The more you know, the more you know you need to learn. Leaders are students of possibility, strategy, innovation and human dynamics. Mostly, leaders are willing to confront themselves to know who they are and what matters to them because that is where the fuse to create something new begins.

Leadership through wisdom takes many forms. Business is an expression of that leadership.

- Street performers who reinvented the circus. (Guy Laliberté and Gilles Ste-Croix, Cirque du Soleil)

- Reimagining working out for women as a short-burst social break. (Gary and Diane Heavin, Curves)
- A trucking chain that initiated training truckers against trafficking, saving lives. (Pilot Flying J, Truckers Against Trafficking)
- An attorney who discovered untested rape kits then led an initiative to track kits using technology and handle backlog for new convictions. (Kym Worthy, UPS)
- A research project to organize the world's information and make it universally accessible and useful. (Larry Page and Sergey Brin, Google)

Each of these cases seems obvious after the fact. And yet, with each one, the leader had to follow their intuition to do something that had not been done to create something that is now accepted as mainstream.

The other key component to success for each of these was seeing the benefit for others as a result of their initiative. After all, leadership that doesn't serve others isn't about leadership – it's about ego.

Obviously, there are many, many more examples of leadership as applied wisdom in business; the more salient point is that you can be one of them going forward.

Risk What Is

When you pay attention to what you know, trust your instincts, get clarity in practical terms of how this insight can benefit others and are willing to risk what 'is' for 'what can be' through action, you are a leader.

While what you know can be perceived as creating change, you may be unwilling or even daunted by stepping up as a leader. However, the real culprit in what holds you back from your leadership is what you know to be true. If you have any confusion, questions or misalignment between what feels right for you, it is hard for yourself, much less others.

The big questions for you are: What do you know? How can it help others? What action can you (as your 25-year-old self) do right now to prepare for a successful future of what you 'know'?

ANNA SARNACKA-SMITH

Anna Sarnacka-Smith is a Master Human Resources Consultant, Business Coach, and a Master Behavioral Consultant. She is the President/CEO of EFFECTIVENESS (www.effectiveness.pl) and an author of "Successful Summiting – Your guide to reaching new heights in business" published on the Polish market.

Anna specializes in evaluating candidates' potential effectiveness during the recruitment process, diagnosing the strengths of existing employees and their leaders and using DISC D3 (DISC/TEAMS/VALUES/BAI) competence tests. She train teams in the scope of the skills they actually need to meet their goals, prepare development plans to advance their skills and later evaluate the results.

Having worked for top Public Relations agencies, Anna has been able to share with Clients my expertise in building client relationships, selling projects, team leading, hiring and crisis management.

Linkedin profile: https://www.linkedin.com/in/annasarnackasmith/

Chapter Seven

Asking for help reveals strength, not weakness

Advice by Anna Smith

Sometimes, I imagine myself as an already older and well-experienced woman. I am in my cozy home, sitting comfortably in an armchair, sipping hot, aromatic tea. I turn my gaze towards a large window. There is calmness behind it and the wind is playing lightly with the leaves on the trees. I'm not in any rush, I can now make time for everything that's important. I can also easily find some time to think about what really matters in life and what's best for me. I reminiscence those fears, convictions that didn't allow me to move forward, live life at its fullest, including my professional life, which I have always found very important. In this vision of mine, I am smiling at my fears, knowing that they had existed only inside of my head and that if I could turn back time (back to my 25-year-old self), I would have tamed them much faster. And the one sentence I would have most definitely told my younger self with full kindness, would be: "Remember, asking for help reveals strength, not weakness".

And even though it may sound so obvious and be so frequently heard from others around us, I am still deeply convinced that putting this truth into practice as self-prided humans, doesn't come easy to us. There are many reasons for that. I have collected them all for you, my reader, by analyzing my experience as well as everything that my employees or clients have experienced. People differ, but as it turns out, when walking through life, we face very similar challenges, which includes being wise and asking for help. I used the word "wise" on purpose, because I want to share with you how you can ask for help without burdening others with your tasks while still taking personal responsibility for your actions. I will share with you how you can ask for help so that you can feel satisfaction and others feel an important part of your success. Are you ready?

Asking for help does not mean that you lack competencies

One of the main reasons why I didn't ask for help in the past was the assumption that if I disclosed that I couldn't cope with something, I would reveal to the world that everything I could or knew was not enough. And although it is true that I don't possess all the possible knowledge on every single topic and I don't have certificates for all possible competencies, how terribly the "what they will think" assumption restricts myself and how terribly it distorts the reality of what they really think.

I remember the beginning of my career. My professional life started with public relations and I stayed within this industry for the 12 years. I can still recall my first tasks. It consisted in preparation of texts for the media about beauty products. Since I was given such a task, I assumed that I must be able to write press releases in accordance with the accepted standards. My superior even asked me if everything was clear. I replied "yes" without any hesitation and got down to work. It didn't even cross my mind while editing the texts that I could admit that I would need some good practices to learn from, in particular with the initial projects; that while working on the project, I could go back to my superior with some questions to verify the effect of my work and be certain that I was heading in the right direction. Instead I came to the conclusion that since I was assigned a certain task, I was supposed to fulfill it perfectly. That is that. To my surprise, my texts needed multiple corrections and I took every remark made by my superior very personally. Willing to impress her and prove in some sense that I was competent, I also didn't allow myself to ask any questions or share my doubts with her at the next attempt. I was in the "I don't need anyone's help" mode with some internal ban on asking for help. As if caught in a vicious circle, I repeated the same nonconstructive thoughts my head: "If I ask, they will find out that I don't know it. And if it turns out that I don't know something, it will be clear that I am not fit for this job. And if it turns out that I am not fit for this job, I can just sit and wait to be fired, etc." Consequences of that situation were emotionally difficult for both sides, since they caused self-disappointment, the feeling that I disappointed others and the feeling of being constantly criticized. I could hardly be clear-headed in that situation, as I was driven by emotions.

I notice similar attitudes in my current employees. Today, 'I know' that asking for help is a proof of strength and when I assign a task to someone, I emphasize that I am there to help them; that I prefer them to ask me questions and ask for help in learning the right direction, to them not doing it and working their tails off trying to prove to everyone around that they can manage on their own. After all, I, of all people, do understand that a new job, new challenges mean that one cannot do everything on their own. I can remember this one new person in my team who wanted to fulfill every task without asking too many questions. This person thought that she must know "it" and that every further question might be a proof that she is not fit for the job. This is when the "I don't need anyone's help" mode keeps creeping in. So, what happened? The first days, a huge number of mistakes were made, and not just minor ones! You can easily imagine how I felt and how much her perfectionism was put to the test. This employee didn't want to ask for help, although she had the person with, an entire baggage of similar experience, at her fingertips. But as it usually happens in life, we first must fall down in order to stand up stronger.

Coming back to my situation, it was the understanding of behavior styles as well as the strengths behind them and fears generating them that marked the real breakthrough in my attitude towards asking for help and is now also the skill, I am teaching my employees and clients. In my case, it was the fear of being criticized. I've put a lot of work into getting to know myself and my own worth. And today, I can easily say what value I contribute to the team. I understand my strengths and respect their power. I am proud of them, because, in this way, it is easier for me to admit that I don't have to be able to cope with everything. Let's face it, I don't have to, and I will not be, just like everyone else in this world. I am a human – created to be a good, but not a perfect one. And this is positive, because it's true. I am aware of my talents, I want to share them with others every single day, but I also let myself learn from others who also have skills to share.

I no longer try to be a hero, but I let myself be me. I talk to myself, explaining to myself that I am the decision-maker here, that I can easily turn problems into solutions and that this is a value which I contribute to my team or clients. Keeping this in mind, I don't let myself forget that there are areas in which I am far from perfect and asking for help in those cases is simply common sense. Today, I put it for example into such words:

- when talking to a client: "I want this training course to make an actual change in your team, therefore I wish to understand the specificity of your industry better. I know that we have already spent some time on it, but I am not certain if I got all the necessary aspects correctly. I would like to ask you for an additional meeting – it will help me with the preparations for the project a lot. What do you say?"
- when talking to an employee: "I know that I communicate in a very task-oriented manner and sometimes even sound

directive. I realize that it is sometimes difficult for you. It is not easy for me to notice moments in which my communication is too dominant for you. I need you to show me the moment in which it becomes difficult for you to talk to me. Would that work for you?"

You need to notice that when asking for help, I keep in mind what value I am offering to the other person. First, I indicate what I am giving or will give myself and then I talk about those cooperation aspects in which I will need support. Rest assured that since I started asking for help in such a way, it has never been badly received. Instead, I always experienced a friendly attitude and readiness to accommodate me with what I need. I show my "human face" this way, in other words, what I am strong at and where I need others, do you see it? What's crucial is that today I consciously give myself the right to not be able to deal with everything on my own, even despite having significant professional experience. There is a chance that I would come up with the thing I am asking for on my own, but is my time worth it? Why shouldn't I invite others to work with me or to a work for the benefit of improving the quality of our cooperation? The answer seems pretty obvious. It is that you need to remember that asking from help is an expression of humility, which shows your current abilities and personality as well as how much is still ahead of you.

Ask for help, but don't demand it

Sometimes the fact that we don't ask for help, doesn't necessarily mean that we don't need it. We need support, but we assume that we simply deserve it or that others should address our needs and give us a helping hand just like that. But it doesn't work like this... If you need help, ask for it openly, instead of expecting that someone will come up with the idea that you need this help. If you don't do this, you may be left with a bitter and often unfair feeling that others ignore or disregard you.

Once in the past I painfully experienced such a situation. It was the time when I had only started learning about my right to ask for help and articulate it clearly. Because, to be clear, I do have this right, but I somehow assumed that since I was so sensitive and could recognize when others might need my help, then those others would also automatically know when and what kind of support I might need. I thought that if someone knows me, then they would not need a university degree to be able to understand my situation. What added fuel to the fire, was a number of "empowering" books, motivational lectures which all emphasized the following key phrases: "You are important, fight for yourself and don't just sacrifice yourself for others" or "your life shouldn't revolve around helping others". So, then a day came when I told myself that I was done with being an "on-call" supporter for others. I would start to consciously expect help from others – both in my private and my professional life. I adopted an attitude which assumed that "from now on" I would change my approach, without telling others about it, expecting that in some magical way they would know when to meet me halfway. Yet, all I got was a cold shoulder and immense frustration on my part. My expectations towards others grew and so did the level of disappointment when I was left to my own devices. This supposed opening up to others and their help shut me off from people and I experienced such bitter loneliness as hardly ever before. I was disappointed, feeling that I wasn't receiving even a small amount of the support which I used to give others every single day.

So, as it often happens with unclear and unnamed emotions which haven't been worked through – they burst out sooner or later. In retaliation for the lack of the "help-related" initiative from others, including my employees, I flooded them with a myriad of unfulfilled expectations. Yet, this time, I had no problem naming everything I had been waiting for, but never received. I talked about how exploited, unappreciated but also hurt I felt. I can perfectly recall that confused look from my employees and friends, with which they tried to tell me: "Anna, it's not like that, we had no idea that you might be needing our help. You, always strong, handling everything perfectly. This is how you carry yourself; this is the Anna we know. If only you had told us right away, we would not have left you on your own".

Luckily, I am the type of person who, after realizing that a certain behavior strategy doesn't work, analyzes the situation, draws up conclusions and names the lesson that have been learned from what had happened. That time was no different. I realized that receiving help requires asking for it and not expecting it. It also requires an attitude based on recognizing that I have others around me who can support me, because I also give them a part of me every day and not because I am entitled to this help. This help is not something I am entitled to because I support others. It can be given to me if I open myself to others, showing them myself in my full humanity, revealing to them that I am not self-sufficient, that there are days or tasks with which I need others and that is alright.

I use this lesson often in my relations with my employees. By modifying the ways of asking for help, I give them courage to trigger similar behaviors. I keep showing them that they're good behaviors and my employees can experience positive reactions which are evoked all by themselves. Once, I confided in my employees and told them that I am really scared of carrying out a training course for a client who has much greater managerial experience than I have. I asked my team to let me present basic ideas and objectives of the training course in front of them, before carrying it out. That's how I function when I'm stressed: it really helps me to have someone with whom I can discuss what I am currently working on. After I have revealed my fears to my team, I heard: "Anna, it's good to be able to get to know you better. On a daily basis, I see you as a businesswoman, consultant, a tough person and now you reveal such innocent experiences to us. I feel like I know you much better, the real you. It's good that you've asked for help, since we wouldn't have thought that you might need it."

Asking for help requires mental training

The fact that I am asking for help today required significant thought training on my part, just like every new behavior which I want to make a part of my everyday life with myself and others. Once I understood that asking for help is a sign of strength, not weakness and that I could find help within others, I needed to work out a habit of stopping negative thoughts about myself. So now, every time negative beliefs start to form in my head, I stop them and check if they have any rational background and if not (and in most cases they don't), then I convert them into a positive thought. Here's an example of how my mental training looks like:

EXAMPLE NO. 1:

NEGATIVE THOUGHT: "You should cope with it on your own"

IS IT REALLY LIKE THIS? "No"

POSITIVE THOUGHT: "I don't have to cope with everything on my own. I can benefit from others".

EXAMPLE NO. 2:

NEGATIVE THOUGHT: "You being where you are professionally, you should really know it by now"

IS IT REALLY LIKE THIS? "No"

POSITIVE THOUGHT: "In order to fulfill a task correctly, I have the right to ask others for help".

Yes, development of positive thinking requires elbow grease, everyday work. It's an obvious thing, but I want to emphasize it, because it so often becomes the reason why we stick to our old habits, despite not being able to achieve our goal that way. I want to encourage you to look at this endeavor not as a curse, but instead as a natural element of a life change, something positive. And we don't grow up out of it. When we were children, it was a challenge to learn how to talk, to walk, and even riding on two wheels is not an easy as pie. It's not all that different when we are adults. Making sure that you give yourself the right to ask for help, in particular if you have not allowed yourself to do it before, requires work from you. Don't wait for something magical to happen and for others to suddenly start reading your mind or for the circumstances to be more favorable. There is a slim chance that anything will happen *just like that*.

I understand that in adult life it is sometimes difficult to take up this work, as no one is forcing us to do anything and we can make decisions concerning ourselves on our own. As kids, we used to shout out our desire to be a grown-up and to do whatever we wanted to. I did it. And when I'm finally this grown-up, it turns out that it's not that easy to push yourself to achieve what you want and need. What can be done about it? Is it worth it to go the extra mile every single time when you feel that the direction you want to follow and the one you need? When observing fulfilled people, please keep in mind that most probably have already made the decision to work on moving in the chosen direction. They considered themselves ready to take up the endeavor.

While browsing the Internet, I found out that a surfer spends only 8% of his or her time "on the wave", 54% rowing and the rest is waiting for the right wave… At first glance, what he (or she) does may seem extremely simple, yet there is a huge amount of work behind that as well as perseverance in repeating the same tasks, in order to be fully prepared for anything a wave might bring when it finally does come. It's hard to imagine a strong surfer who had not made the endeavor to master the art of paddling. I didn't use the word "effort" on purpose, because it has negative connotations for me; in this word I can hear some kind of need to give up one thing for another. Today, I prefer training myself to take the next step towards my goal. Yet, the further I want to go, the more support I need from others.

One more fun fact about surfers. Many beginners position their bodies incorrectly on the board. They usually stand too far at its top and due to that often end up in the water, instead of on the wave. But with time, as they work regularly on their skills with the help of professionals, they notice their mistakes and correct them. And I want to highlight that one aspect: with the HELP. In life, just like in the case of surfers, we must be open to new behaviors, action strategies, which we have not tried before (as simple as that, yet, when you give it a closer look, hardly anyone does it). And since they're new to you, the most efficient step towards your goal will be using the help of those who have already gone down that path. Thanks to that, you will be able to grow and catch every possible "wave". It will let you stand out from mediocrity.

I don't ask for help because I want to control the situation

As we grow up, we seem to lose this "helping" vitality, the courage to reach higher, to ask for help. But when we were children, it was natural that in order to see more, we had to ask others to lift us up. And then the world looked differently, gave us much more possibilities. We didn't worry what others would think, we didn't assume that we had to take the first steep steps solely on our own. We simply asked for help. Over time, we became entangled in loads of unjustified beliefs, fears and assumptions convincing us that if I am a grown-up now, I need to have control over my life. And when I ask for help, does it mean that I lack this control? On the contrary...

In my head, I often return to childhood experiences and when I analyze them, I find two truths which are so important to me:

1. **When you live life at its fullest, there is no place for perfective verbs:** I possess, I achieved, I finished. There is only place for: I have, therefore I can want more, I carry out, go further in the chosen direction, but without one specific goal, I am open to everything, because if I know the taste of satisfaction, then it is possible that there is something much more exciting waiting for me around the corner; that if I know what it means to accept myself, then I will soon be able to truly love myself; that if I have already found that love, then it is highly probable that someone will soon love me more than anything; that if one tea tastes exquisitely, then maybe it's worth trying out other tastes, because I can find something even better. And going further this way, if I think of something in a certain way, then most probably I will at one point change my mind and it will also be fine; that if I feel regret towards someone, then there is still a chance that it will go away and that I will accept everything that this person has done to me, as part of my experience and I will work through it in order to move forward. And if I want to move forward, then it's even better if there is someone by my side who will support me and whom I can ask for help without any remorse.

2. **When I ask for help, I still have control over my life**. I have learned that if I come across a closed door and I can't get through, then I look for another one, instead of just standing there and continuing to knock on that one door, hoping or expecting that someone will finally open it just because I'm still there. I have regained good control over my life by taking that control from the little voice steering my life: "what I can do, what I can't do, what I will let myself do and what is out of the question".

Summing up, asking others for help doesn't deprive you of control over your life – on the contrary. If asking for help has not been your good habit so far, remember you can always change it. As already mentioned, new behaviors require perseverance and, obviously, the courage to experience new things. And sometimes experiencing new things is very difficult and you think that it will hurt, that someone will criticize you or reject you. You're afraid of losing your security. Don't worry, everyone experiences fear. Allow yourself to think that it's alright to feel like that. Look, we all give ourselves permission to lose comfort in various everyday situations. We don't bring into question that a new pair of shoes causes temporary discomfort. Reaching out to others and asking them for help may also be linked to a short tension, because you experience something new and you don't really know what to expect. Don't worry, acknowledge this feeling and remember that even if you don't *like* the new thing, you can always go back to your well-known behaviors.

Ask for help – you will live a better life this way

Asking for help is good. Look at it as a powerful tool that you have at hand in order to make progress in life. You can reach high places all on your own, but at what cost? Why shouldn't you reach for something even higher enjoying the support of others? Remember, asking for help doesn't mean or doesn't have to mean burdening others with your tasks. It's the wisdom and strength of benefiting from those who are better than you in a certain field. Get out of this "I don't need anyone's help", "I can manage on my own" cage of yours. Look for mentors who will help you grow, share what you're good at with others and indicate the areas in which you need their support. This is a good path which will bring you much higher than you could ever get on your own. After all, this is what life is about, isn't it?

ROBERT EVANS WILSON, JR

Robert Evans Wilson, Jr. is an award-winning writer and speaker, who works with companies that want to be more competitive through innovation, and with people who want to think more creatively. A world-class storyteller, Rob is the author of the internationally syndicated column on innovation, achievement, and leadership: ***The Un-Comfort Zone*** which runs in *Psychology Today* (as *The Main Ingredient*) and more than 300 other publications. He is also the author of four books including the inspirational book: ***Wisdom in the Weirdest Places***; the psychological mystery novel: ***...and Never Coming Back***; the humorous children's novel on dealing with bullies: ***The Annoying Ghost Kid***, and the hilarious, illustrated collection of bathroom graffiti: ***OFF THE WALL! The Best Graffiti Off The Walls Of America***. For more information, please visit RobWilsonSpeaker.com.

Chapter Eight

Ask More Questions

Advice by Robert Evans Wilson, Jr

After parking the time machine outside of my apartment on Eighth Street, on the day after my 25th birthday, I ring my doorbell. It's a Sunday, and the timing is good because the only time I ever lived alone was for 18 months between the ages of 24 and 25. I was also opened to letting strangers into my home. I say this because I recall an incident that will happen later on this year where I let a man into my apartment who I didn't know. He rang the doorbell and when I answered, he asked if I recognized him. I said, "No, but come on in, and we'll figure it out. Want a beer?" It turns out that wasn't such a wise idea. He was the ex-boyfriend of my girlfriend, and he came to threaten me if I didn't stop seeing her because he wanted her back. I tried to have a rational discussion with him, which was naive on my part because what could be more emotional than a matter of the heart. I eventually had to order him out of my apartment. He then used a screwdriver to punch holes in my gas tank to prevent me from driving to her place. Hmm, perhaps I should make a mental note to warn myself about that incident while I'm here today.

I pushed the doorbell and decided to use a similar tactic as my future tormentor. As I open the door on myself, I say, "Hi Robert, do I look familiar to you?"

I look at me and reply, "Uh, yeah, are we related?"

"Indeed, we are. May I come in?"

"Please do."

I walk over to my favorite chair and have a seat, while my younger self stammers, "Um, that's where I sit!"

"Oh, but I have missed this chair so! Your future wife is going to make you throw it out."

"What!"

"Yes, Robert, I'm you from 37 years in future. And, I've come back in time to give you some advice."

I watched myself stand there and absorb the situation. I was always a big science fiction reader, so I saw myself recover quickly, "Cool! Like where to invest money?"

"I'm afraid not, although what I came to tell you may very well help you become wealthy."

"Okay," I replied while sitting on the sofa, and giving me my complete attention, "I'm all ears."

"The main thing I want to tell you is to ask more questions."

"Questions?"

"Yes, you've learned from studying philosophy to be a good critical thinker, but you need to apply it more often."

"What do you mean?"

"Critical thinking is a bigger part of creative thinking than you currently realize. You know when you attend the movies, how you frequently have to engage in a willing suspension of disbelief because it enables you to accept implausible scenarios and enjoy the show. How it keeps you from yelling, "No way!" at the screen when you see a revolver fire more than six shots, when car thieves always find the keys on top of the sun visor, and when a paperclip can pick any lock."

"Yeah, I know what you mean."

"The trick is not leaving that suspension of disbelief at the theater door. Innovators and creative thinkers willingly suspend disbelief - all the time. It enables them to imagine airplanes and telephones and Game Boys..."

"What's a Game Boy?"

"Uh, never mind, you'll find out soon enough. The objective is to let your imagination run free and look for connections everywhere. Imagining the fantastic will free you from the boundaries that would otherwise contain you. It enables you to pursue ideas that others think are unattainable. That artist you like, M. C. Escher, who does all those fun drawings of preposterous structures, once said, "Only those who attempt the absurd will achieve the impossible.""

"Cool quote, I'm gonna have to write that one down." I watched myself pick up the legal pad and pencil off the coffee table, which was always nearby to write down any ideas I might get and start jotting.

"One of the cardinal characteristics of creative thinkers," I continued, "is their willingness to abandon the traditional ways of viewing things. They question authority and challenge the status quo. They ask questions like: Why do we do it this way? Is there some other way to do it? Why can't we try it another way? You should be asking these questions all the time about everything."

"All the time! About everything?"

"Yes, even when things are going well, you don't want to stop questioning authority or challenging the status quo because there's always room for improvement. Whether it is your business or your personal life, asking questions may enlighten you to problems before they occur."

"That sounds exhausting!"

"It may be at first, but over time it will become automatic like a habit. Here's an exercise you can do that will help stimulate creativity: ask how you might use an object for a purpose other than what was intended."

I look up from my note pad, and into my eyes, and ask, "Could you give me an example?"

"I like to pick up items at random sometimes and try to imagine a new use for it. It can be a real use or a fantasy use, the purpose is to exercise your creative-thinking. A pot from the kitchen could become a helmet, your pencil could be a weapon for stabbing, the television could become a two-way communication device..."

"Yeah, I've got a paranoid friend who already thinks it's watching us back."

"Ha Ha, I remember him. Another exercise is to take two objects and imagine combining them into something new. Say a can of Coke and an ink pen."

"I know what we'll call it: The Soda Fountain Pen with drinkable ink!"

"There you go! Keep doing that with all sorts of things and eventually it will become second nature, and before you know it, you'll be conceiving all sorts of new inventions."

I continue, and say to my former self, "I know that you're already committed to constantly learning and adding to your store of knowledge. I still adhere to what you learned from the Greek philosopher Socrates that learning is a lifelong process. When he was found guilty of teaching his students to question authority, he was given a choice of punishment: death or exile. He chose death, stating, 'The unexamined life is not worth living.' One of the best ways to examine life and increase your knowledge is to ask journalistic questions."

"Journalist questions?"

"Yes, and I like to recite a Rudyard Kipling poem to help me remember them: 'I keep six honest serving-men (They taught me all I knew); Their names are What and Why and When And How and Where and Who.'"

"Ha Ha Ha!" my younger self laughed, "I'll remember that!"

"I know you will," I laughed back. "Asking what, why, when, how, where, and who, will guide you to find everything you'll ever want to know and more. And, those are important questions when it comes to critical thinking. They will help you avoid scams. I can't remember when I did, but have you read any Oscar Wilde yet?"

"Yes, *The Picture of Dorian Gray* and *The Importance of Being Earnest*."

"Well, Wilde once said, 'The world is divided into two classes, those who believe the incredible, and those who do the improbable.' I've always interpreted that quote to mean that gullible people will believe any ludicrous lie that's told to them because they aren't critical thinkers; and that the creative thinkers who question the ways of the world will produce the next generations' inventions and innovations."

"Who is telling all these ludicrous lies?"

"You've heard the joke, "How do know when a politician is lying?""

"Yes, when his lips are moving."

"Unfortunately, that will become more and more true. And, the liars will also come to include the media and even scientific researchers."

"Wow."

"You've heard the Edgar Allan Poe quote, 'Believe nothing you hear, and only one half that you see.'"

"Yes."

"Well, with future technology, Poe's warning will only get worse. One way you can be on the alert is the more sensational a story seems, the more red flags you should look for. Oftentimes politicians, special interest groups, and their sympathetic media will take a minor story and blow it out of proportion in order to distract you from some other more important story. You will have to be eternally vigilant in order to find out what to truly believe."

"Give me an example."

"I've been trying to avoid telling you about anything specific that is going to happen, but this is as true now as it will be in the future. Never underestimate the motivation for money and power. Everyone already knows right from wrong: don't kill, don't steal, don't lie, don't initiate force, don't harm anyone in any way, so how many laws do we really need to enforce that? If you look deep enough, you'll see that pretty much any new legislation will have a money trail. In other words, some people are going to benefit from the law at the expense of other people."

"Again, how about an example?"

"You can do your own research, but I will share one with you only because it affects your health. Sugar is cheaper to grow in the Caribbean than in the states, so US sugar growers bribed Congress to tax the cheap imported sugar to make it as expensive as domestic sugar. That tax caused many food product manufacturers to switch to corn syrup. I learned this the hard way in 1987 when I drank a soda that had made the switch. I had a severe allergic reaction to it and had to start reading the ingredients on every processed food product I eat."

"Wow, thanks for the heads up!"

"Let's get back to how important critical thinking is. It's about forming a judgment. It is about examining and evaluating information that you have received. Testing it, applying scientific methods, and interpreting it. However, you also need to be aware that your judgments will be influenced by your personal motivations, such as beliefs, assumptions, and experiences. In order to truly become a critical thinker, you must become aware of your biases. You must ask yourself, 'Do I have the integrity and humility to question my own prejudices?' If so, you can be much more objective in your assessments."

"My biases?"

"Yes, they affect your worldview. You interpret the world with what you know until you learn otherwise or find evidence to the contrary. Sometimes your mind will correct the actual things you see in order to match your worldview. I can't tell you how many times I've proof-read something I've written only to completely miss errors that seem glaring when someone else finds them. My mind reads it the way I think I wrote it. The cure comes by reading it aloud; I seldom miss errors that way."

"Wow, you're right, I do that all the time. I'm gonna write down that I need to proof-read aloud."

"I don't recall that you've ever read anything yet by the German writer, Johann Wolfgang Goethe, but he said, 'We see only what we know.' That thought makes me wonder what else in the world we are not seeing that is right in front of us. I've heard stories of isolated native peoples, who have never been exposed to modern technology, being shown photographs. The natives could not make sense of the two-dimensional pictures, even those taken of things they knew. I've also heard that Pacific islanders could not see the big sailing ships of the early world explorers when first exposed to them. At best, some saw the sails as large white birds."

"I remember hearing that, too."

"Let me make this bias concept more personal. I know you remember how frightened you were by Aunt Doris's pretty bottle with the blue fluid inside."

"Do I ever! I was four years old, and I'd been making mud pies with Paul, when Aunt Doris told us to wash up for lunch. We walked into the kitchen, and I saw Rafe leaning against the wall, shaking and crying uncontrollably. His face was red and wet with tears, and he had a line of drool hanging from his open mouth. I was shocked. I couldn't imagine anything that could make Rafe cry. He was big and powerful; twice my size and twice my age, he was the first older boy I had ever been associated with. I remember asking him if he was hurt, and he just mumbled incoherently. Then his brother Frank, the one between Paul and Rafe, said, 'He isn't hurt; he said a bad word, and Mother washed his mouth out.' As a four-year-old, I couldn't conceive of what that meant. I didn't know what a bad word was, nor had I heard of having your mouth washed out. But, from the look on Rafe's face I knew it must be horrible and I was terribly frightened. A few days later, I was watching Aunt Doris clean the bathroom. On the counter I saw a beautiful glass bottle with a bright turquoise liquid inside, and I thought it might be something tasty like *Kool-Aid*, so I pointed to it and asked, 'What is that?' Aunt Doris replied, 'Mouthwash.' And, I ran screaming out of the room."

"And, why did you scream?"

"Because I didn't know that mouthwash could mean a breath freshening rinse; the only thing mouthwash meant to me was a poison for punishing boys until they cried."

"In other words, your worldview had been biased to only believe that mouthwash was something bad?"

"Yes."

"And, your biases can make you miss all sorts of things simply because you don't have the worldview to see it. You should ask yourself how your rigid political or religious beliefs might be preventing you from seeing alternatives that are obvious to others. Isaac Asimov, I know you've read him, said, 'Your assumptions are your windows on the world. Scrub them off every once in a while, or the light won't come in.' It's like clearing clutter from your closet or desk - it opens up space for new things to come into your life. I interpret that 'light,' Asimov is speaking of, as all the new connections you'll be able to make, the new ideas you'll be able to form, when you expose yourself to information, you're not familiar with."

"But, how do I know that what I believe is prejudice and not fact?"

"By reading a lot and exposing yourself to new information. It might even make you a little uncomfortable to research contrary opinions, but they will put you in touch with your feelings and help you understand what your own motivations are in the opinions you keep. Best of all, the new information you uncover will prepare you to recognize opportunities you would never have imagined otherwise. Go on open that publication that makes you cringe and read, read, read."

"Ha Ha Ha!"

"I also want you to question the motivation of people who want to come into your life for various reasons. There are times when you are too trusting. It could be someone trying to sell you something... like another multi-level marketing scheme."

"Ha Ha, yeah I'm on to them now."

"Even people who you wouldn't assume having a profit motive should be questioned."

"Like who?"

"Like any professional such as a lawyer, accountant, dentist or a doctor; experts aren't infallible, so it always pays to get a second or third opinion. Anyone whose authority you've been trained to automatically accept, should be questioned."

"I get it, like finding an honest mechanic to work on your car."

"Or it could even be someone who wants to be your friend or wants to date you. They may have a hidden agenda."

"Like that pianist I was friends with last year. I was just getting into classical music, when I met him at the record store. I knew he was gay, but that didn't bother me, I believe people should be free to be whatever they want. I simply enjoyed hanging out with him. I thought he was cool. He taught me so much about music. I loved listening to him play piano. We even went to the symphony together. I thought we were buds, but then one day he told me he didn't want to see me anymore if I wasn't interested in dating him. I was shocked because I had already told him I wasn't gay. But he was adamant that he wasn't interested in any relationship with me that did not include sex. I was really bummed out."

"He was giving you plenty of clues, but you just missed them. In his mind, you were already dating. Again, it was your worldview - as a heterosexual - that kept you from seeing it. Until you question motivation more, it will happen again. Another example, and this isn't really telling you anything about the future, but there will be a woman who schedules an interview with you on the pretext of hiring you, when all she is really doing is trying to start dating you."

"Hire me to do what?"

"That would be revealing too much about the future that still needs to unfold for you. The lesson is to question people's motivation if anything seems off. Don't ignore your feelings and trust your gut. And, here's a biggie I need to share. You've already learned this to some degree, but you really need to learn it better, otherwise a lot of people are going to take advantage of you."

"What is it?"

"Actions speak louder than words. You are very trusting of other people, so you are still wooed by words over actions. Too often you take people's words at face value. You are a pleaser, you always want to make sure whoever you are with is happy - especially the women - even at the expense of your own happiness."

"And, why do I do that?"

"Because you don't think you're worthy of being treated better."

"What!?"

"Not believing you're good enough has defined your entire life."

"Now wait a minute, that's just not true."

"Okay, then tell me why you became an Eagle Scout?"

"Because I wanted to."

"But why? You weren't looking for approval from your classmates at school, you never wore your uniform to school, and hardly anyone there knew you were even in Boy Scouts. No one in the troop you stayed with the longest became an Eagle while you were there. You weren't trying to impress your fellow scouts, and none of the scout masters were aware of what your rank was until you applied for Eagle. So, what was driving you to get it?"

"I thought it was cool to reach the top."

"I say you did it to impress Mom and Dad."

"No way, they weren't pushing me to get it. I got no encouragement from them at all. They weren't like those parents who told their sons they couldn't get their driver's license until they earned their Eagle. Mom and Dad never even attended the award ceremonies. Dad was never involved with the troop like other dads were. All he did was drop me off and pick me up, until I was old enough to drive myself."

"Still you got it for them more than you got it for you."

"How do you figure?"

"You're not looking deep enough. When I was little, I recall Mom and Dad always talking about how impressed they were with the sons of their friends who earned their Eagle. They would go on and on about it. It planted a seed. A seed that if I became an Eagle, I would be good enough, I would be worthy, and they would love me."

"Well, of course, they loved me."

"There's no 'of course' about it."

"What do you mean?"

"Let me ask you this, can you explain why you were bullied so much in elementary school? You didn't fit any of the categories of kids who are usually bullied. You were attractive, you had no physical flaws, you were one of the taller boys in your class, you made good grades, you could run faster than anyone in your grade, and you could hit a softball over the fence, and yet you were always chosen last when it came to being picked for teams."

"Yeah, it never made sense to me. I couldn't understand why the other kids would call me names or pick fights with me."

"It was nothing you did, but the other kids could sense something about you from the way you carried yourself. That you were insecure and afraid. Bullies love that because they are also afraid and insecure. When bullies find someone, who is more afraid than they are, they will attack that person because it makes them feel powerful, and the more powerful they feel the more secure they feel."

"Okay, that's true, I was terrified of that school from first through third grade, and then around fourth grade I got over it."

"What were you so afraid of?"

"I was afraid of the teachers and their paddles, and principal and his paddle, I was afraid of getting spanked for no reason. And, I was afraid of the older students in the upper grades because some of them picked on me."

"Then what happened?"

"When I was in fourth grade, I stopped being afraid of the teachers and the principal because I realized they wouldn't arbitrarily spank me for no reason."

"But before that you felt like the world was an unpredictably evil place. Why was that?"

"I don't know, I guess because I was young and stupid."

"No, there is an actual reason. It was because I - you - grew up in an unstable household. Mother was an emotional basket case. She was unpredictable, and I could get in trouble for anything that happened to displease her. What was okay one day, was not okay the next. Mother was volatile; I never knew what to expect. I couldn't understand that old saying about not crying over spilt milk, because anytime I spilled milk, Mother would yell at me until I was in tears. She could be happy and laughing, or sad and crying, or angry and yelling. Her lack of emotional stability was a type of abandonment. She was never there for me or Cindy. She was completely wrapped up in herself: her singing, her hobbies, her clothes, her hair, her tan. Remember the time she forgot to pick me up after day camp, and I sat in the rain at the bus stop waiting for three hours. I was scared and crying, I was only six years old. She never remembered. Dad came home from work and asked where I was. It was only then that they came to pick me up."

"Oh yeah, I was so scared that day, I'll never forget it!"

"Dad might've been a better parent, but he was a victim too. He was so caught up in trying to please Mother, that he never had the time to focus on Cindy and me, or even his own needs. You see, at home, you - I - grew up in an unstable world that seemed capricious. It took me until about halfway through fourth grade to realize that the world is not unstable and capricious, that the world has rules, at least the school had rules, and I couldn't be punished for doing nothing like I could be at home. Once I realized that, I felt like I had some control, and I was no longer afraid."

"I remember fourth grade being the year I quit being afraid of school, but I never knew why."

"Homes can be unstable for a variety of reasons: narcissism, alcoholism, neglect, abuse, and divorce. All of those can lead to an unsound environment for a kid. These situations constitute emotional abandonment and the child does not feel safe. He will never feel good enough, and that insecurity may keep him from trying to experience new things throughout his life. Nor can a child growing up in these conditions develop the self-esteem and self-confidence necessary to stand up for himself, to protect himself from bullies."

"So, you're saying that I was bullied at school, because I was bullied by Mother at home?"

"Yes. A child who grows up in a stable home with loving, supportive parents becomes confident and poised; and has inner-strength to face the world and not be afraid of it. And, they are unlikely to be bullied."

"Wow, do I become a psychologist?"

"Again, that is something that I cannot tell you."

"Okay, you said, 'narcissism.' I've heard that word, and I've always thought it referred to someone who was fixated with the way they looked, but you make it sound like it is more than that. What is it?"

"Now you're asking the right questions. I didn't learn what narcissism really is until I was in my fifties. And, learning about it is probably the most important thing I've ever learned."

"How so?"

"Because I found that I was attracted to narcissists, and they to me."

"So, what is a narcissist?"

"A narcissist is someone who feels like he or she is special or more important than they really are. They want to be admired by everyone. They believe they deserve special treatment over others. They are quick to envy those that have more than them. They are obsessed with appearances, their beauty, their clothes, their homes, and that of those with whom they associate. They can be obsessed with success which makes some of them great at business. Or they can be obsessed with power, which is frightening because it attracts them to government. They are users and takers; they befriend people for what they can get from them. And, the biggest characteristic of all is that they lack empathy. They don't care about anyone beyond what that person can do for them; and when that person is no longer able to give them what they want, they will drop them like a hot potato with no regrets."

"Wow, that's much worse than I thought. And, much of what you said describes Mother. I remember her telling me I should be friends with some kids because they had a pool, or horses, or a trampoline, not because I liked them. And, she used to send me to spend time with her rich friends and telling me to show interest in their hobbies."

"Ha Ha, that's right, and clearly I didn't do what Mother expected because none of them lavished me with wealth!"

"So why is Mother that way?"

"It's generational, but I believe it is learned and not genetic. Mother's father was a narcissist, and so was his father. Dad's mother was a narcissist which is why he was attracted to Mom."

"Are you saying I'm attracted to women who remind me of Mother? Eww!"

"More specifically, women who behave like Mother. It's how you were raised; it's what you know, what you're familiar with, and what you're comfortable with. When you meet nice giving women, who treat you well, it just feels wrong to you because of your bias that women are supposed to be selfish and taking. And, narcissists are attracted to you because you are a pleaser who is giving, and you are likely to meet their demanding needs."

"Well, that explains the woman I was dating about a year ago. I broke up with her when I found out she was cheating on me, but here's the part I couldn't understand, afterward I still wanted her. I was still extremely attracted to her. And, now I that I know what they are, I can see that she has a lot of those narcissism traits you described."

"That's what I'm hoping to spare you. That's why I came back in time. You keep dating women who treat you like crap, yet you hang in there hoping they are going to treat you better. But they never do. Narcissists are incapable of love. You can never do enough for them to make them love you. Oh, they'll say they love you, but always remember - actions speak louder than words. Some psychologists have described my attraction to narcissists as a subconscious need to correct my relationship with Mother, that deep down I believe that if I can get another narcissist to love me, it will repair my unrequited love."

"That's freaky."

"The reason that you are - that I am - a pleaser is because you were raised by a narcissist. You need to look very carefully at the people to whom you are drawn. Your goal should be to live an authentic life for yourself."

"How can I do that?"

"One way is to only keep things and people in your life that bring you joy. You see, many of our fears as adults were formed when we were babies, or toddlers. That's why I encourage you to question your own motivation - why you do the things you do. Then dig deep and discover the fears that are directing your life. Because if you can find those now as a young man and learn to control them, you will be able to do so much more with your life. Even things that seem obvious to you might turn up different answers when you question deeper. For example, why do you want to be a writer? Peel back that onion and see what comes up."

"You're kidding?"

"No, you might be surprised. Okay, one last thing before I go. Ask questions about your genealogy."

"My what?"

"Your ancestry, your family tree."

"Why?"

"One day you're going to want to know, but the longer you wait, the fewer people there will be who can answer those questions."

"Is someone else going to die soon?"

"That's not what I'm saying, but the further out you go on the branches of your family tree, the more people you will find that are gone and are no longer available to tell you family stories. The sooner you start, the more older family members you'll get to meet and learn from. It was through my genealogical research that I figured out that narcissism was generational."

"So, I'll learn about family traits?"

"Yes, and so much more. You'll learn about all sorts of interesting and exciting people in your family history."

"Where do I start?"

"With everybody who is still alive."

"I asked Mother once, but she didn't seem to know much."

"Oh, she knows a lot more, you just need to ask more questions."

"And, asking more questions is what you came back in time to teach me."

"Yep, well I better get back to the future. I'm curious to see what will have changed because of our little visit here today."

"Ha Ha, are you scared?"

I nod and reply, "A little."

Marcus Aurelius Anderson

Marcus Aurelius Anderson is a Bestselling Author, TEDx Speaker and International Keynote Speaker, High Performance Mindset Coach for Leaders, CEO's and entrepreneurs. He's also the host of the #1 New and Noteworthy podcast "Conscious Millionaire Epic Achiever" show.

While preparing to deploy with the U.S. Army, Marcus suffered a severe spinal injury that left him paralyzed. After dying on the operating table twice, the surgeons saved his life, but told him he'd never walk again.

Having no other option, Marcus started doing some brutally honest soul searching, looking for the lesson to be learned from his injury. Once he started seeing his Adversity as a gift instead of a curse, something miraculous began to happen... Marcus now speaks, coaches and inspires others to overcome their own Adversities to actualize their personal definition of success in business and every area of life. His message teaches how we can use our own Adversity to make us into better leaders, citizens and human beings to positively impact the world.

CHAPTER NINE

"KNOWLEDGE UNUTILIZED IS THE EQUIVALENT OF IGNORANCE."

ADVICE BY MARCUS AURELIUS ANDERSON

They say that "youth is wasted on the young." Of course, we never understand what that truly means until we've misspent some of our youth. The reality is that anyone can repeat wise words, but to truly understand them takes life experience.

The advice I'd give my younger self would be moot because at such an age, I'd be too short sighted to understand the value of such words. It would be pearls before swine type of scenario. Yet, I will humbly attempt to write some words of wisdom to my younger self from my current vantage point of life and experiences.

Advice is never in short supply. There is plenty of "experts" giving advice seemingly all the time, much of which is based largely on theory and conjecture. I'd like to point out that it's very easy for someone to sound like an expert when there's really no way to test the information being spouted.

To be frank, the advice I'd give my younger self goes against the current vogue. Everyone preaches the notion to "learn as much as you can every single day." While that sounds altruistic and enlightened, it is not necessarily useful.

My advice would be to stop learning. Hear me out.

It is very easy to consume knowledge passively but another thing entirely to put it into action.

Going to the most prestigious colleges, attending the best training events, and learning from the most successful people in the world is all well and good. However, to be exposed to such knowledge without implementing it would be a huge wasted opportunity. Knowledge that goes unutilized is the equivalent of ignorance.

Instead of trying to find the latest and greatest advice, I would recommend putting the knowledge you already possess into action. While this seems simplistic, it must be. Once you're in the heat of the battle, complexity quickly unravels and betrays your best efforts.

From all my years and experience of coaching countless clients and consulting for companies and teams, these are the most common patterns of human behavior I've seen emerge. These are the things most likely to stop someone from putting information into action.

Lack of Priorities

In 2012 while preparing to deploy with the U.S. Army I suffered a severe spinal injury. During the surgery that followed, I flatlined on the operating table, twice. Though the surgeons were able to bring me back to the land of the living, when I woke up in the ICU I was told that I'd never walk again and that I'd be paralyzed for the rest of my life.

Everything went sideways and I went into a deep, dark, suicidal depression. I literally wanted to take my own life but was unable to act on it. Laying in that bed for months gave me a tremendous amount of perspective. I was filled with anger and regret. I was livid with myself for wasting so much of my life. I realized that

I'd wasted so much time, talent and potential on thinking that I'd always have the time, talent and potential to do whatever it was that I wanted to do. During this time, I did some brutally honest soul searching. This made me realize that I'd done many things in my life that weren't even what I really wanted. I understood that I was doing these things for other people. In other words, I was replacing my priorities with the priorities of others.

I use my story as an example of the importance of prioritizing the right things. If we try to make everything a priority, then nothing becomes a priority. This keeps our efforts and focus spread thin while watering down our efforts and impact. If we don't have priorities, then our efforts simply meander down the path of least resistance. Having the wrong priorities keeps people from acting on the things that are truly worthy of that effort.

Excuses

This is one of the biggest reasons people fail to get started. Our time is finite, but our excuses are infinite. People will point to lack of resources, lack of information, or lack of skillset when trying to explain away lackluster results. But there are other things people use as excuses that they don't even realize. Perfectionism is one such excuse. For Perfectionists, they need to have the entire plan mapped out perfectly to the T in order to move forward. Even when well planned, the endeavor still seems too overwhelming creating "analysis paralysis." The biggest excuse is that people fear failing in front of witnesses; therefore, they continue to seek even more information in hopes of gaining clarity and save potential embarrassment. The reality is that more information simply muddies the water and makes decision making more laborious. This reinforces the default setting of hesitation and inaction. These things lead to even more excuses.

Don't get caught up in the semantics of the "how" of execution and simply start right now, right where you are this very moment. Starting is the hardest part. The reality is this: The answers you seek will be found in the lessons learned from the failure of your attempts. Even the best laid plans will go astray to some degree. Instead of allowing this to slow you down, look for opportunity in the chaos of execution. As for the witnesses who see you fail, remember this: The loudest boos always come from the cheapest seats.

Feelings assassinate the truth

Some won't take even the best advice because they have a prejudice against the source. There are countless belief systems, philosophies and dogma attached to knowledge, it has been that way since the dawn of man. Each of these schools of thought want to be the 'authority' in their respected subject, many wanting to have a monopoly on Truth.

Because of these segmented mentalities and teachings, it is easy to nitpick the source of information you disagree with. For example, imagine a lifechanging quote or piece of information you've read that was so powerful and profound that it absolutely struck you to the core. Now, imagine the source of that knowledge was a person whose political and religious belief were diametrically opposed to your own. Would you be able to divorce your feelings and judgments of that person from the powerful truth they just revealed? Could you still see the unadulterated facts of their words or would you have the equivalent of intellectual "sour grapes" and try to find holes in the information they gave, eventually throwing it away and not using it at all? This is the very definition of Cognitive Dissonance.

The quickest way to learn anything is to be able to absorb Truth and Knowledge irrespective of source. In my experience, neither side of any political or philosophical argument is completely correct. Each side will have pros and cons. By being open to all possibilities, you can avoid the pitfall of chasing your tail dictated by dogma. You must understand that if you simply throw away valuable information because you don't agree with a portion of it or the source, it is you who suffers from your folly. In addition, anyone you could help with this information suffers as well. Don't let your ego get in the way of your edification.

They are "special"

Some will do the opposite of demonizing the source and instead put the person who gave the advice on a pedestal and make them "special" and untouchable. By doing this it makes the source's advice and results unattainable for anyone else. This is of course a cop out. You don't get to simply call someone else extraordinary and sit on your hands while you still possess all kinds of unactualized potential.

The person giving you the advice from their experiences is human. This means they are fallible and have failed many times in their efforts. It's much easier to look at a person who is successful in a certain arena and make them out to be uniquely gifted and talented than to look at all the hard work they put in to get to that point. Because by acknowledging those facts, it also means we must acknowledge that we can reproduce the same results if we are willing to put in the same amount of work as well. This leads us to the next reason.

Lack of work ethic

If you've seen the work ethic of any successful person, you will see that they are simply willing to outwork everyone else in order to succeed. Period. This is true in business, entrepreneurship, sports and any other competitive endeavor. While this doesn't mean that they grind 24/7 until they burn out, it does mean that when it's time to put in the work, they do so without hesitation.

Everyone wants to "work smarter not harder" but the reality is those at the top of their fields do both. They are continually learning to be efficient and work smart while working hard at it. I've found that those who only want to work smarter and not harder are usually those with the most questionable work ethic to begin with.

When I was in the military there were hardships put before us every day. Adversity was an inevitability. I learned quickly that if I simply stopped resisting the hardship and work that was necessary to achieve the objective and went forward with my best efforts, I saved myself a lot of headache and heartache. If you are at war internally about why you have to do something arduous or monotonously telling yourself, "This is stupid, why do I have to do this?!" or "I HATE doing this!" it wastes mental energy that would be better spent focusing on the goal at hand. Stop resisting the idea that it will be difficult. Come to the realization that it absolutely will be difficult to make your goals come to fruition. Once you accept that it will be difficult, ironically, it will become easier.

I've heard that before

The great Stoic Seneca said famously, "It is impossible for a man to learn what he thinks he already knows."

If we're honest, we've all been guilty of thinking "Yeah, yeah, yeah I've heard that before." We then judge the information as useless and discard it without a second thought. However, just because you've heard something before doesn't make it less true.

When you study any subject matter long enough, there will eventually come a place where there is some overlap regarding information. Many believe that if the information they're getting isn't something completely new to them that it's not worth listening to. There have been countless times when I've learned a tremendous amount about material that I was very familiar with by simply emptying my mind of what I thought I knew about it and listened intently with the desire to learn. You must understand that if you've heard the same piece of advice from those whom you respect and are incredibly successful, then that wisdom bears repeating. And if you've heard it over and over and it isn't working for you, take a moment and re-evaluate your execution. 99 % of the time, the fault is in the way you've interpreted the information, not a flaw in the information itself.

That seems too easy, it's got to be more complicated than that

Many people think that the more complex something is, the better it must be. While this intellectual subterfuge may keep them mentally occupied, it does little to help them take action. People associate complexity to represent "more" while they think of simplicity as "less." And most people by their very nature want more than less. Just because something is simple doesn't mean it's necessarily easy. Indeed, understated elegance and complexity is found within the overlap of simplicities.

Keeping only a few key ideas and principles in mind makes execution not only more focused, but it makes it easier to take action in the first place. The more options we have regarding anything, the longer it takes for us to make an informed decision. By trimming the fat and keeping things ruthlessly simple, it helps multiply all efforts and create tremendous momentum.

They try to do what successful people are doing now

Because there is so much information at our fingertips today, it's easy to Google information about anyone who is successful and find out more about what made them successful. But this can be misleading.

For example, many people forget that the mega successful entrepreneurs like Ed Mylett, Gary Vaynerchuck and Tom Bilyeu have been working hard in their businesses for literally decades. It's very difficult to expect a person with only a couple of years of experience in business to take what is working for these legends now and expect it to work for them. For example, the aforementioned entrepreneurs don't answer their own emails, phone calls, or most of their own social media, they have a team that does that for them. So, while at their high level of success they have gradually built themselves into a position to be able to do that, it would be tough for someone just starting out to "hire out their weaknesses" in every regard like these entrepreneurial giants can. The same goes for understanding how and where to apply their monster work ethic. At the multimillion-dollar level, those who are successful have developed an instinct to know when to go all in and apply their entire focus on a project and when to save that effort for another time.

People don't respect what they don't pay for

When I coach other coaches, I often have to re-iterate this lesson. There is something in our human nature that causes us to not respect something that we didn't have to pay for in some way, shape, or form. Ask yourself, do you value something that you got for free as much as something that you paid top dollar for?

As a coach, entrepreneur or service provider, it's imperative to charge what you're worth. The dynamic regarding this is involved but absolutely worth exploring. For example, let's say I coached someone for free. Chances are at the beginning of the coaching relationship things would go well. But as a coach, we don't really begin to earn our money until after the client has lost their initial enthusiasm of the process. When the client is now feeling the hardship of doing the work and thinking of throwing in the towel is when true coaching begins. Unfortunately, if the client isn't paying anything for the coaching, they aren't truly committed. Because they don't have any "skin in the game" they will do what they've done every other time they faced the hardship of changing behavior; they'll quit.

There is but one level of commitment; and that is total. That's why it's imperative to charge what your worth as a coach, entrepreneur or service provider because now every client that you have will be fully committed to you and the process. When they are committed financially, that provides leverage to keep them engaged and makes them take your coaching to heart. Without skin in the game, the client doesn't really take your coaching seriously. Here's the other side of the coin.

If you aren't charging what your worth and you have a client who you sense isn't going to put your coaching advice into action, then subconsciously as a coach, you hold back. You hold back because you don't believe they will act. The client feels this as well, and now what little commitment they did have evaporates when they sense that you are "phoning it in" as a coach. This becomes an unhappy marriage where neither party can win. The client will not sing your praises and refer you other great clients while the client will not receive the life changing coaching that they deserve because of the compromised coaching. Here's another important reason to not maintain this type of coaching relationship.

As a coach, if you are working with a person who doesn't take you seriously, this lowers the bar on your coaching skills. In other words, instead of improving and coaching to the best of your ability, you're actually becoming worse as a coach because of these bad habits formed from your noncommittal coaching style.

The reality is if people don't pay, they don't pay attention.

I use the coaching example to make this point because many people don't want to pay for advice, they want it for free. They don't want to invest in themselves by investing in quality advice, therefore, all the "free advice" they are getting is subpar at best. But because this is advice they haven't paid for, that they aren't committed to, even if it was the best advice on earth, because they don't respect it, they likely won't act on it. This is an excuse I see time and time again. To an employee in a company, even if the company has spent hundreds of thousands of dollars on the employee's training, the employee doesn't always take the training information to heart, because to them it was free. And people don't respect what they don't pay for. Thus, the vicious circle repeats leading to more frustration for all parties involved.

Disbelievers

There are also those who are simply disagreeable by nature. People like this are continually trying to play the "what about this?" game. They will listen to some valuable information and pragmatic tactics and then say, "Well what about if X happens?" Even when given a correct and thorough answer, they will come back over and over with countless other "what about this?" scenarios. This indicates that they likely don't know enough about the subject to understand the value of the information being presented. They are literally not qualified to have the misguided opinion that they have and are simply trying to sound intelligent by being argumentative. While I'm very open to Devil's Advocacy, eventually it becomes tiresome and useless.

The goal isn't compelling enough

People will often start with great expectations. These expectations are usually dashed the first time they run into Adversity and hardship. If there isn't a compelling reason to achieve the goal in the first place, then they will lose enthusiasm and quit trying eventually. When they started, they liked the idea of achieving the goal, but in actuality, they just wanted to see if they could achieve it without having to put in too much effort. Once it becomes obvious to them that it will take significant sacrifice and commitment, many stop completely.

Goals and desires can also change as time goes on. Situations and priorities often shift in life. A person who is married and has children will often have different priorities than a single college student might. These changes of season in life can make a goal become less or perhaps even more compelling depending on how things evolve. Outgrowing of a goal or finding that the goal no longer serves them is another reason why people stop taking action and stop working towards a goal.

Lack of accountability/deadline

Without a deadline, time means nothing. This is a simple reality that explains why some people hesitate to take action. Because they don't have something holding them accountable in some manner, many people stay complacent. And complacency leads to mediocrity. *Parkinson's Law* states that "work expands so as to fill the time available for its completion." In other words, if something is due in two weeks, people will procrastinate until a few days before to get it done. But if you give them a two-day deadline, even if it's difficult to do, the deadline will give them the urgency to make it happen. When it comes to acting on the information that someone already possesses, few will seek out someone to help them with accountably. This explains why you see so many people who go to the gym regularly, yet they look the same year after year. However, if a person joined the gym knowing that they were in a competition in 3 months, that would keep them motivated. They would reverse engineer what they would need to do to reach their best condition and constantly try to reach new levels with each of their workouts. They'd also clean up their diet to the best of their ability to set themselves up to succeed. Having a coach, personal trainer or even a committed workout partner are all great ways to keep focused on taking action on the information you already possess. People don't need more time; they need a deadline.

No metric to measure effort or outcome

Along the same lines as above, most people are much too vague about their desired goals and outcomes. A goal is only as attainable as it is specific and by not taking the time to do the work and ask themselves the hard questions now regarding what they want, sets them up to drift aimlessly having to constantly pivot and change course for somewhere they have no clue where to reach. Having a general idea of wanting to make more money is a common example of this. If someone truly wanted to make more money, they'd have a more specific goal such as "I want to make $20,000 a month." This very specific metric gives a target to shoot for. Having this goal in mind, we can now reverse engineer and find out how much money needs to be made each week and break it down into days or even hours. This goes hand in hand with the idea of accountability and having a deadline. By having a specific metric to measure the goal combined with a timeline creates a laser focused vision on what action steps need to be taken. This is what helps mobilize people to take action.

Conclusion

Addressing only a couple of these issues will help more people begin to execute on their goals. Addressing all of these issues one by one will help a team, company or organization become much more efficient, effective and productive as well.

All of this material harkens back to my original notion of taking action with the knowledge you already possess. People often don't give themselves enough credit and always assume everyone else knows more than they do. But when given the chance, these same people who think they have nothing of value to add know a lot more than they even realize. By looking at these shortcomings in black and white, it takes away the emotion and fear associated with hesitation and lack of action. This suspends personal judgement and shaming, freeing them up to be creative and think in a manner that sets them up to succeed in every possible capacity.

Bruce Lee said, "Knowing is not enough, we must act. Willing is not enough, we must do." I couldn't agree more. The moral of the story is to stop searching for that magical "missing piece" of information and start executing now on the knowledge you already have. The reality is there is no finish line in and that we will always be incomplete in some way. Once we can accept this, we can begin to focus on what we know instead of constantly berating ourselves about what we don't know. Chances are that if your back was against the wall right now, you'd have a pretty good idea of at least a place to start. Even if you didn't, you'd likely know how to gain the information to find where you'd like to begin. When I think back to myself at 25 years old, I realize that I'm only now beginning to relearn and rediscover some of the things that I took for granted back then. Indeed, I'm having to unlearn many habits to get back to the level of simplicity of my younger self. Of course, I'm able to have these opinions only after years of trying multiple things in order to come to these conclusions. The magic you seek is in the Adversity that you're avoiding.

ROCKY ROMANELLA

Rocky Romanella was born New York City and raised in New Jersey in an Italian family. He began a 36-year career with UPS on June 15, 1976 as a part time loader and unloader. From there, Romanella climbed the ranks to become President and General Manager of UPS Supply Chain Solutions and President of Global Retail Operations where he led one of the largest re-branding initiatives in franchising history; The UPS Store, revolutionizing the $9 billion retail shipping and business services market. After retiring from the largest transportation and logistics company in the world, Romanella went on to serve as Chief Executive Officer and Director for UniTek Global Services, a mid-cap telecommunications solutions company. Today Rocky is the Founder and CEO of 3SIXTY Management Services, a company that specializes in Speaking, Leadership Development and Consulting Services. Rocky is one of the best keynote motivational speakers in the country and internationally. He has spoken in large and small venues all over the US including cities like Atlanta, San Diego, Las Vegas, Phoenix, NYC, Dallas, Chicago, Miami, Houston, LA, Charlotte and many others. Internationally, some of the cities, Toronto, Mexico City, Milan, London, and Krakow. He creates excitement through his energy, passion and knowledge. He will connect with your audience, regardless of size, in a one to one conversational style. Rocky will paint a picture through his unique storytelling as he delivers his Motivational Keynote Speech.

CHAPTER TEN

BUILD YOUR LEGACY
ADVICE BY ROCKY ROMENALLA

INSPIRED BY "LEADER OF THE BAND" BY DAN FOGELBERG

An only child alone and wild, a cabinet maker's son
His hands were meant for different work
And his heart was known to none
He left his home and went his lone and solitary way
And he gave to me a gift I know I never can repay

Daniel Grayling "Dan" Fogelberg (August 13, 1951 – December 16, 2007) was an American singer-songwriter, composer, and multi-instrumentalist, whose music was inspired by sources as diverse as folk, pop, rock, classical, jazz, and bluegrass. He is best known for his 1980 hit "Longer" and his 1981 hit "Leader of the Band".

After 48 years of dedicated service Pasquale Romanella finished his work, cleaned his station, shook hands with a few coworkers and exited Creative Steel Rule Tool and Die Company for last time. He left with no plaque, no card, and no retirement party – just with gratitude - thankful to have worked in the same place for 48 years after migrating to a new country at the age of 14. Hardworking, Loyal, Dedicated, Family man, Thoughtful – those are words that could be used to describe my father.

I always felt bad for him; I thought he deserved so much more recognition. A short time after he had retired there was no prouder moment in my life than when I was able to present to him my 25 Years of Service watch at Thanksgiving Dinner. To me there was no better way to honor him and thank him for instilling in me and our family the values and ethics that were so important to our successes.

It was those values and ethics that defined me, defined how I lived my life, and ultimately how I defined my leadership style. Over the course of my business career, primarily at UPS, I always wanted to honor the legacy of those that came before me. In my case the single most influential person that came before me was my father – but I was also influenced by others and in my adult life, my wife Debbie is my greatest influence.

I always admired George Washington. If I could go back in time and have a diner with one person, George Washington is always my answer. It is not because he was a great general, or our first president, I always wanted to ask him the question, "How did you motivate and inspire your troops to stay, fight and remain loyal against all odds?" During my 36-year career at UPS and later during my tenure as CEO I met, worked with and learned from some amazing people, too many to thank but all influential. To all of them, I say thank you.

I'm just a living legacy to the leader of the band

What is your LEGACY?

In creating your own legacy you are trying to honor the legacy of those that went before you. With this in mind, your starting point may actually be your finish line. It is who you want to be at the end of your journey that actually sets the course for the journey. To help in our legacy journey and conversation, I have chosen the song, **Leader of the Band, by Dan Fogelberg** to highlight and identify our leadership roles and responsibilities as we create our legacy. I believe his thoughtful lyrics can breathe life into our conversation.

Here is your first challenge, think of the word you would want people to use to describe you at the end of your career. We are all unique, so what are your hands meant to do, what is the word that best describes what is in your heart and soul as a leader. The word that best describes your brand. Is it hardworking, dedicated, loyal, energetic, aggressive, decisive, thoughtful, respectful? This is just a small sample of the words that can be used to describe an individual and their brand idenity. Once you have selected the word that you would like to describe your career, this word will sit atop your hall of fame leadership plaque, and will define your brand and your brand promise. Your word is your bond, so choose it wisely. It will define you and your career. Word of mouth is still the best advertisement, it will be the word used to describe you and the brand experiences people had with you.

> *A quiet man of music, denied a simpler fate*
> *He tried to be a soldier once But his music wouldn't wait*
> *He earned his love Through discipline*
> *A thundering, velvet hand His gentle means of sculpting souls*
> *Took me years to understand*

I have been very fortunate through my career to have had the opportunity to work with, learn from and mentor some incredible people. I often get asked for advice, encouragement and suggestions as individuals are beginning their career and or reflecting on their careers. As I think through the many people I have encountered, and they come from all walks of life, they do have some traits and skills and beliefs that make them more similar than dissimilar. Although I do not profess to be an expert, I am a lifelong learner who has been shaped and influenced by some outstanding people at all levels. So, let's take a look at these traits, attributes and skills and together we can build a skills inventory that you may want to use as you perform your legacy analysis on yourself.

I believe it starts with Values. It is what you do when no one is watching that counts. Integrity can often be used to describe this activity, but I would like to take it further, it is the integrity of your word as well as your actions. I think the integrity of our actions is something we can grasp and to which we can relate. But what do I mean by integrity of your word, simply put, you make a commitment to follow up on something, respond to a request, commit to an action and you do it!

I believe that two fundamental ingredients of a successful person are hard work and enthusiasm. There is no substitute for Hard Work and an equation that I believe successful people use is…. Time + Effort + Enthusiasm = Results. Enthusiasm is what fuels your drive and keeps the engine revving. Without enthusiasm your equation is time and hard work, and although these are two important ingredients to success, always remember hard work without enthusiasm is just that… HARD WORK. Hard work by itself gets old!

Another way to look at it is…. Make it Fun. Make it Happen. But, above all else, Make it Happen Fun! Finally, I believe we should all ask ourselves some key questions and answer them with a critical eye, with honesty of purpose:

- How can I add value in this current position and going forward?

- Do I have a process mind with a strategic vision and the ability to execute tactically the strategy?
- Can I develop a strategy, build a business plan and execute that plan?
- Can I provide clear communication and walk the talk?
- Can I teach my teams to learn to take better control of their day and balance multiple priorities, measuring and following-up for continuous improvement?
- Do I accept the responsibility for my results?

"My brothers' lives were different for they heard another call
One went to Chicago and the other to St. Paul
And I'm in Colorado When I'm not in some hotel
Living out this life I've chose and come to know so well"

All of our lives are different, and where we are from where we started will be different for all of us and in many ways a measure of our success. But living out this life "I've chose and come to know so well" will be your final measure of success. It will help keep you grounded throughout your journey and true to yourself, your values and your mission. A successful leader can be summarized as a person who adds immediate value as a trusted advisor, mentor and visionary who uses a process approach to lead the organization and its people to new levels of success. Great organizations need to have a thoughtful vision and strategy. Great leaders need to combine that strategic vision with the ability to execute the strategy tactically and effectively assess:

1. Who am I?
2. What do I stand for?
3. What won't I compromise?

This is your brand and your brand promise, your legacy. So lets talk about legacy and the legacy journey in a pragmatic way.

There are many ways to define success. I believe the ultimate definition of success will be in the answer to the question **"What is your Legacy?"**. I subscribe to a simple but powerful definition. For me it was always about the answer to the question. Did you leave things a little better than you found them? More broadly and from a business perspective;

- Are your people better because of their time with you?
- Are your customers better because of their interactions with your company?
- Are the shareowners and stakeholders better because of your influence and stewardship of the company?

As you grow and develop, take on new challenges or simply move into a new phase of your life, you will be faced with complications and adversity that may set you back. Honesty, perseverance, and trustworthiness will become major factors in overcoming these obstacles and creating your personal brand and your legacy.

Along the way, you will come to a decision point or stage gate. Your choice is simple but profound in each instance, but a decision must be made. Your choices are to **LEAD, FOLLOW, or GET OUT OF THE WAY.** If you choose to lead you will need to be an honest and trusted leader to establish your vision, mission, and values so that those in your care or supervision will trust you enough to follow. As a lifelong learner, you are constantly forging a path to transform yourself into a high-character, high-performance leader. You will never be without challenges both in life and business. But if you are focused and ready to face these complex business challenges and personal changes with discipline, determination, honesty of purpose and in an ethical manner you will be successful.

He left his home, and went his lone
And solitary way, and he gave to me
A gift I know I never can repay

Whether we realize it or not, we are all here to determine what our real intent is in life. For each of us it may be different. For some, a great spouse, father, mother, leader, or mentor but all will want to have a legacy of leaving the place a little better than they found it. Purpose driven people put their morals, character, and honesty first. Without purpose, we drift. With purpose, we steer. You have a responsibility to yourself and to others to use your best judgment, weigh your options carefully, and make the right decisions, even if they're not the most favorable or popular, even when no one is watching! When you do that you honor yourself and your values. Wherever your path takes you, know that your trustworthiness is your highest honor. For if you are a trusted leader, others will believe in your vision, mission, and values and will trust in you enough to follow you.

That will be your legacy. As a person, your core beliefs are not what you would like them to be, but rather what lives and breathes in you as a person. The good news is that you will have many opportunities in your career and in life to demonstrate these values and beliefs, but one chance to get it right each time.

With this sense of responsibility, we are constantly in pursuit of the knowledge whether written or experienced on how to be a good leader and how we improve our skills. We take great pride in the books we have read and where they sit on the bestseller list. I often found that some of the best examples and learning experiences come from the people we have met, the experiences we share and our openness to learn from these experiences we have along the way. These experiences help to develop EQ and creativity and nurture growth and develop our personality and social skills. These are all skills we aspire to and are trying to develop as leaders along our legacy journey. These interactions provide us the opportunity to respond and develop our own opinions about topics but within the guidelines of right and wrong and moral and ethical behavior.

Leaders must develop EQ along with their educational intelligence and business acumen. Sometimes a simple conversation or the simple but powerful words from Dan Fogelberg "***My life has been a poor attempt to imitate the man I'm just a living legacy*** *to the leader of the band"* can help us see the bigger picture, promote moral and ethical behavior and maybe, not take ourselves so seriously that we lose sight that it is not always about us, but it is about them, the people in our care.

The **Leader of the Band** sets the tone from the top. He or she is the leader, role-model, mentor. As the leader, we define our vision and commitment towards openness, honesty, integrity and ethical behavior from a values perspective.

Consider a company's mission statement. The mission statement for a company is defined as, "An official document that sets out the goals, purpose, and work of an organization." A clearly defined mission statement can help the leaders of an organization strengthen the company culture through a unified sense of purpose, helping the team, and the organization improve decision-making with clarity and purpose supporting the big picture.

The leader must enhance cross-functionality and relationships through a shared understanding of priorities. Put another way, everyone in the band must understand their roles in creating perfect music. The leader must articulate the vision for the organization.

As the leader we must define the optimal desired future state, and articulate and describe the mental picture of what the organization wants to accomplish over time.

He or she provides guidance and inspiration as to what the organization is focused on achieving in the future. Everyone in their care (the Band) must understand their role and what they are working towards every day because it ultimately contributes towards accomplishing the goals and aspirations of the company and the Band. Finally, the leader must succinctly write and speak to be inspirational in a manner that makes it easy for all employees to understand "what good looks like."

This clarity helps everyone in the organization to understand and articulate the big picture and the vision of what we do, who we want to be, and how we want to do it. The leader will set the tone and through his or her leadership style and brand promise will maintain honesty, integrity and ethics. The leader will live the value and mission statement and will not silently sanction bad behavior. We are more likely to uphold these values and principles when they align with our personal values and ethics and the organization is in sync with its people and policies and all are playing from the same sheet of music.

The **Band Members** represent leaders in the organization at all levels. The management team must clearly communicate the company's ethics, values and mission throughout all areas of responsibilities at all levels. It is unacceptable to make statements like, "Corporate said". When a leader or band member makes these types of statements, they give away their authority and send the wrong message to others they lead.

The values can be communicated in many ways through meetings, informal gatherings, one-on-one communication or the informal day-to-day operations. Regardless, they must be things that everyone can articulate upon request and emulate when the opportunity presents itself.

An only child Alone and wild
A cabinet maker's son, His hands were meant for different work,
And his heart was known to none

Maybe another story can help bring clarity to this thought of how you as a leader choose to see things and create your legacy:

Three people were laboring in a field of boulders and large stones. Sweat ran from their foreheads as they swung their heavy picks again and again. A curious passerby approached them and asked each what they were doing.

- The first person answered in a stern and abrupt voice: "Can't you see, I am breaking rocks!?"
- The second person replied in a matter-of fact way: "Can't you see; I am earning my salary!?"
- The third person smiled-their eyes gleaming with enthusiasm and proclaimed: "Can't you see, I am helping to build a Cathedral!!?"

Leadership is not a passive duty it is an active responsibility. It is expected that the Leader of the Band leads. This means providing everyone in their care the leadership they need to successfully reach their destination. You have a responsibility to model effective leadership along with honest and ethical behavior to the employees you represent. Open and honest communications and visibility are an important element of trust. Make sure you are available to your people and visible in your operations or department so that your people know what we are trying to accomplish even if it is unpopular.

The statement "My **life has been a poor attempt to imitate the man"** represents each of us as we try and learn from the leaders, peers, friends and experiences as we create our living legacy. They are the many good people who work with and for us.

Regardless of whom you are at that moment in time, the leader of the band, member of the band or the audience, I believe all will play an important role that will help you to define your legacy.

These elements, mission statement, values, ethics, procedures and practices and the tone from the top, are in place to help meet and exceed the vision for the organization in all facets of the Business. Your role, whether it is as the leader, member of the band or audience continues to be that catalyst for change; the person who understands, accepts and lives the mission and emulates the values in all you do. The result of these actions will be a great company, organization or family providing great service that we all can be very proud of and a great leader we can all follow with a living legacy that others will want to emulate that will define our career and your character.

"I thank you for the kindness, And the times when you got tough". As we move through difficult periods on our way to success, I want you to keep this thought in mind as you engage with your customers and work with each other, "Do the 'right thing' rather than 'things right'". Take care of your customers, treat each other with dignity and respect, celebrate your successes and your reward will be "a rich legacy." - a person that we are all proud to say we worked with and for. A recognized brand (legacy) that others will try and emulate, and a person people will want to follow willingly.

The leader of the band is tired, and his eyes are growing old

But his blood runs through my instrument, and his song is in my soul

The heart and soul of a person's legacy is in the essential ingredients of great leadership and interpersonal skills. These ingredients became the foundation of the brand promise and will help to create the living legacy of the leader of the band. Here are the essential ingredients. Ask yourself in the privacy of your own heart and conscience where you are on your journey and how would you answer these questions:

1. Do I deserve the respect of the people in my care, my peers, my boss, my family, friends and those I have relationships with?
2. Do I treat them with dignity and respect?
3. What are the things that I do to be helpful to them?
4. Do I view them as part of the solution or part of the problem?
5. Do I take the time to understand some of the issues that may be affecting them and their performance?
6. How carefully do I listen?

7. Finally, am I viewed as a person who is sincere, fair, honest and impartial as a leader and person?

A person who may be technically qualified but with poor "people relationships" will be ineffective. We all have deficiencies in our relationship skills, but by recognizing them and trying to overcome them, each of us can make improvements. We should remember at all times to be courteous and pay attention to the details, as these details can mean a lot to those we interact with and can become the fabric of our legacy.

I thank you for the music, And your stories of the road
I thank you for the freedom, When it came my time to go
I thank you for the kindness, And the times when you got tough
And, papa, I don't think I Said I love you' near enough

The Rest of The Watch Legacy

As I have often said, I have been very blessed throughout my personal and professional life to have the opportunity to meet, work with, learn from, and mentor some incredible people. But no one was more influential in my early life than my family and parents—especially my father.

My father was born in Italy and moved to the United Sates at the age of 14. My dad stayed in high school only through his freshman year before leaving school and getting a full-time job as a tool and die maker in New York City.

Although we were proud to be Italian, my father was very happy to be in the States, and very proud to be Italian American. I grew up in the same two-family house my entire life until I moved out when I got married. My family lived upstairs, and my aunt, uncle, cousin, and grandmother lived downstairs.

We had a very family-oriented life and almost every weekend had relatives over the house. My father instilled in all his children the values of hard work, integrity and respect. My parents and aunt and uncle never spoke about money or how tight things were, only that you have one family and make sure you take care of each other because nothing comes before or between you and your family.

I always believed that we were very fortunate to be raised in an environment where you were taught respect. You could disagree, but you were not allowed to be disagreeable or disrespectful. And we were taught that money did not motivate you, achievement did. The measure of your success was based on your success relative to your expectations. You achieved your success the old-fashioned way: you earned it through hard work.

I was blessed to land my first job with UPS – a company that provided a lifetime of career opportunities through its "promotion from within" culture. We have policies and codes that define the character of our people. It was an honor to work for a company known for its people and meticulous business processes that still today shape the culture and character of their global workforce. It also helped to shape my character and reinforce the values that I learned in my house growing up.

As one of our founders, James E. Casey said, "Determined people working together can accomplish anything." Families working together can overcome anything if they support each other and stick together. You still see this character embodied in the actions of UPS'ers worldwide.

My Dad also supported the promotion from within policy without ever really knowing it. It goes back to the conversation I had with him prior to starting my first job as a part time unloader in the Edison, NJ facility. As we sat around the kitchen table and I was describing the job, my Dad gave me the advice that has guided me throughout my UPS career. My dad looked at me and calmly in his own way said, "Rocky, in everything you do, be the best you can be. You owe it to your family. Learn everything you can about your job, and then learn some more. Whatever they ask you to do say, 'yes and thank you for the opportunity.'"

So, every time I was asked to move, I always thought back to my Dad's advice and I said yes. My father believed you lived your values. Growing up, my father would emphasize," It is what you do when no one is watching that counts."

The years of service watch and the story of the watch has great meaning in our family. The story starts with my father's retirement. After 48 years of working in the same shop in Manhattan, my father retired without a card, plaque or fanfare. He was fine with all of that as he was a quiet, unassuming man and grateful for a career that allowed him to provide for his family.

I always felt bad for him. I thought he deserved so much more recognition. When I received my 25 years watch I was so proud, but I thought I would never have accomplished this without the guidance and example set by my father. To me, there was no better way to honor him and thank him for instilling in me and our family the values and ethics that were so important to our successes than to present him with my watch.

At Thanksgiving dinner, I presented my Dad my 25-year watch as my way of saying thank you to him for all he had done for me and as my recognition of his successful career.

He wore the watch every day and shortly after receiving the watch began a battle with cancer. Through all the chemo and radiation, he never took the watch off. When I received my 30-year watch, with the new UPS logo, I presented that watch to him celebrating the fact he had battled cancer for those 5 years.

The original watch, we gave to my son Rocky for his High School graduation to symbolize passing the values from generation to generation. My father was alive for that and so proud to have him wear it in his honor.

My lessons on respect, leadership and integrity from my Dad went deep and wide. In a small but powerful way, the watch was a reminder to live your values.

Dad passed away more than twelve years ago, after his struggle with cancer. Through a difficult time, my Dad never lost his dignity and respect for others. His gentle smile and comforting eyes were his signature style to the end.

After his passing, we presented my son Andrew the 30 year watch I had given my father and like Rocky, he wears it with great pride. They are both ***a living legacy to the leader of the band.***

A little piece of their grandfather is always with them, guiding them to do the right things when no one is watching!

At UPS and the Romanella family we have a legacy, to leave the place a little better than we found it.

We have the responsibility to ourselves and to others to use our best judgment, weigh our options carefully and make the right decisions—even if they're not the most favorable or popular, even when no one is watching!

When you do that you honor yourself and your values. Wherever your path takes you, know that your trustworthiness is your highest honor. For if you are a trusted leader, others will believe in your vision, mission and values, and trust in you enough to follow you. That will be your legacy.

Leadership is something we all have concerns about. Leadership is a concept that is not reserved for, and only applies to, certain people in business, government, and civic organizations. The reality is no matter our age, gender, occupation, educational level or position in life, each of us touches and influences other lives. Through this extension we are all leaders to someone at some time. It can be a person under our supervision or care, a spouse we honor and live with, or a child we nurture, a student we teach or a player we coach. It could be as simple as a fellow member of our church or religious affiliation, club, league or association, but it is usually identified by the fact we have made a positive difference through our actions and examples, we have left our legacy mark.

Integrity can never be taken from you; it can only be given away. Don't ever give it away.

Live your Word Leave a Legacy Wear Your Watch

<u>**Dan Fogelberg**</u> **– Leader of The Band Lyrics**

An only child
Alone and wild
A cabinet maker's son
His hands were meant
For different work
And his heart was known to none

He left his home
And went his lone
And solitary way
And he gave to me
A gift I know I never can repay

A quiet man of music
Denied a simpler fate
He tried to be a soldier once
But his music wouldn't wait
He earned his love
Through discipline
A thundering, velvet hand
His gentle means of sculpting souls
Took me years to understand
The leader of the band is tired
And his eyes are growing old

But his blood runs through my instrument
And his song is in my soul
My life has been a poor attempt
To imitate the man
I'm just a living legacy
To the leader of the band

My brothers' lives were different
For they heard another call
One went to Chicago
And the other to St. Paul
And I'm in Colorado
When I'm not in some hotel
Living out this life I've chose
And come to know so well
I thank you for the music
And your stories of the road
I thank you for the freedom
When it came my time to go
I thank you for the kindness
And the times when you got tough
And, papa, I don't think I
Said I love you' near enough
I am a living legacy to the leader of the band

Deborah L. Smith

Deborah L. Smith is a life coach that assist the needs of others in achieving their long-lost goals, dreams and desires. She is an advocate for women lost in relationships and assists in giving them the strength in getting to their next stage in life. Most of Deborah's career has been spent in the Public Safety career field working as an Emergency Medical Technician, working in a branch of the Arkansas Fire Academy. She is a Past President of the Arkansas Emergency Medical Technician Association and represented her career field by serving as President of the National Association of Emergency Medical Technicians for two terms. Deborah is currently working on a mystery novel with plenty of twists and turns.

CHAPTER ELEVEN

"WHEN YOU CHANGE THE WAY YOU LOOK AT THINGS, THE THINGS YOU LOOK AT CHANGE" - WAYNE DYER

ADVICE BY DEBORAH KNIGHT

1. Begin the lifelong journey of Introspection and Transformation

You have already begun the journey of introspection, the first step to knowing who you are and learning how to keep your self-confidence at its highest level. Take the time to write down all the aspects of you. For example, I am kind, I am interested in learning things in this life that will allow me to find peace, both in my life and in my spirit, I do not like to exercise, and the list continues. Spend time inside your mind to find and catalog all the facets of your personality. When looking inward, be honest, loving and kind with yourself. Just as you should never judge another person, neither should you judge yourself. No facet of yourself is to be judged 'good' or 'bad' as you take stock of your emotional/spiritual self. An ongoing review of yourself is an honest way to learn your values, your goals, your ever-changing concept of what is your "I have arrived!!' moment.

2. Do not seek validation or adoration from other people

When you came into this world, you were blessed with beauty, wisdom, self-confidence, purpose and a knowledge of your value. All the 'right stuff' to allow you to create your perfect life, resulting in a life filled with purpose, excitement and happiness. Work every day to accept all facets of your personality. Realize it is dangerous to look to others for validation of your self-worth. To seek authentication of your true self from others in your life, diminishes your power, your confidence and your desire to move forward with your hopes and dreams. Allowing others to ascertain your value, will cripple you emotionally and cause you to be less than you were intended to be, for people can be jealous and cruel.

3. As best as you can, eliminate procrastination from your life

Do not allow procrastination in your life. Once you have determined there is a task to be done…. then do the task!

The first task I would suggest, is to plan your tomorrow, today. Advancements in technology have created a vast number of programs and electronic equipment that will enable you to handle this suggestion quickly and efficiently. The method of documentation is irrelevant, what is crucial, is your commitment to complete this task every day!

Review of your past entries will also serve as a way to evaluate your time management skills. The review will show you the division between your professional commitments and personal activities. Was the division as you had hoped; or was there greater work time spent versus family and personal time? To neglect either division of time is an indication that the balance you seek in your life has not been achieved. Just as nature strives to keep balance in the real world, so must you strive to keep balance in your body, mind and spirit.

One of the facets of your personality is that you require an extended amount of solitude. Your alone time is needed so that you may reflect on the issues in your life. Conflicts in your life will require a mental massage, so that consideration of all the components may be accomplished and possible solutions brought into being. Memories, both pleasant and somber, will attempt to fill your alone time. Allow them to come to you so that you may languish in the warmth and love of certain memories, review how a different outcome might have come to happen in a less than engaging memory and laugh out loud at those slapstick memories from days gone by.

Your alone time may also be used to take an stock of where you have arrived in your journey of personal and spiritual growth to gauge where you are in obtaining your desired goals, to see if your current goals could do with a bit of rethinking and possible new ones developed.

Alone time can also be the perfect time for a mental recess, whereas techniques such as meditation, yoga or taking a nap can be implemented. Sometimes, just the simple act of quieting your mind is a tremendous relaxation technique.

4. Words and their usage create the movement of your life. Learn which ones can move you forward and which ones can completely change the journey

One of the most important activities you can add to your life is movement each and every day. Swimming has been your choice of exercise for many years. Swimming is low impact, the type of exercise that works well with your body. I would encourage you to continue your swimming outings as often as possible. Those days that do not allow a trip to the pool could perhaps benefit from the inclusion of Ti Chi or walking on a treadmill.

As the saying goes 'a body in motion stays in motion' and as your body continues to age, you will be happier and healthier because you made some form of exercise a part of your daily routine. A walk outside to be part of the beauty of nature, and even though you never have been able to dance, try a 'Dancing to the Oldies' routine. Put on the program and dance away the time. Taking a dance class with your partner is another way to keep moving, plus who knows, it might lead to romance and other enjoyable pursuits.

The battle to combat depression has been a very real part of your life for years. Medical science has proven that exercise produces natural endorphins that aggressively fight symptoms of depression. These endorphins will allow a reduction of your current meds and will help keep your mental outlook brighter and your body able to keep on moving!

Creating beautiful outdoor flower gardens and tending to potted plants is a large part of your summer outside activities and as such provides you exercise and a beautiful landscape. Adding beauty to the world by word or deed, is always an appropriate action. See the beauty of life that unfolds before you each day, the magic of a child's laughter, the sights and sounds of nature are free to enjoy any time and any place. Fun and laughter shared with people you like, or love will keep you young and happy.

"I learn something new every day!" should become your mantra. Keeping your mind active is just as important as taking steps to make sure your body does not become sedentary. Take a class at the community college, learn a second language, and make a list of things that you find interesting. Do a search on the internet to learn more about what intrigues you. If you are not able to take a trip to Bora Bora, then read about the location and customs of the island, there are always beautiful pictures to enjoy, so that you have a visual image of a place, far away, that speaks to your heart.

You have long known the power of your thoughts and words upon your life. Continue to study and learn how words are the current of your life. Words that you use, or think, are what brings into existence your dreams and your heartbreak. Learn how to use words to create prosperity and how to avoid using terms that call emotional drought to your life. Use your words sparingly, especially when you are angry, for once in motion words cannot be recalled and there are always results to follow.

The authors of the bible wrote in Proverbs 18:21 "Death and life are in the power of the tongue." Writer Deepak Chopra wrote "Language creates reality, words have power. Speak always to create joy."

Years of life transpired between the creation of each of these quotes, however, the subject matter is still consistent. You began speaking years ago, and are at this time, beginning to study how thoughts, words and deeds impact your life. Be diligent in your study and un-daunting in your research. There are so many life changing things for you discover, but you must take seriously the search.

As Shakespeare once said, "There are more things in heaven and earth, Horatio, than are dreamt of in your philosophy." Concepts and designs of many of our past visionaries, which were believed to be unattainable or improbable, have, with time and the continued forward thinking of these visionaries, have been proven and their unbelievable designs have now been developed into work saving devices, towering skyscrapers and beautiful artwork.

There are many famous people who spend their lives educating people about the power of their thoughts and words. For example, Dr. Bruce Lipton states, "you can live a life of fear or live a life of love. You have the choice! But I can tell you that if you choose to see a world full of love, your body will respond by growing into health. If you choose to believe that you live in a dark world full of fear, your body's health will be compromised as you physiologically close yourself down in a protection response".

Dr. Lipton is telling us how our thoughts and words have a direct impact on your body's health. The use of thoughts and words are the catalyst for events in your life, for that reason I implore you to expand your study of how we impact the quality of our lives with the responsible language and the consistency of our thoughts.

In the beginning of this chapter I started it with a quote by Dr. Wayne Dyer "when you change the way you look at things the things you look at change". This once again stresses that the thoughts give us the power to see our situations through different lenses. Here is a poem that I read often and reminds me the beautiful way to approach life. Keep these thoughts close to you and read them often, making them part of your life.

Desiderata - Words for Life

Go placidly amid the noise and haste,
and remember what peace there may be in silence.
As far as possible without surrender
be on good terms with all persons.
Speak your truth quietly and clearly;
and listen to others,
even the dull and the ignorant;
they too have their story.

Avoid loud and aggressive persons,
they are vexations to the spirit.
If you compare yourself with others,
you may become vain and bitter;
for always there will be greater and lesser persons than yourself.
Enjoy your achievements as well as your plans.

Keep interested in your own career, however humble;
it is a real possession in the changing fortunes of time.
Exercise caution in your business affairs;
for the world is full of trickery.
But let this not blind you to what virtue there is;
many persons strive for high ideals;
and everywhere life is full of heroism.

Be yourself.
Especially, do not feign affection.
Neither be cynical about love;
for in the face of all aridity and disenchantment
it is as perennial as the grass.

Take kindly the counsel of the years,
gracefully surrendering the things of youth.
Nurture strength of spirit to shield you in sudden misfortune.
But do not distress yourself with dark imaginings.
Many fears are born of fatigue and loneliness.
Beyond a wholesome discipline,
be gentle with yourself.

You are a child of the universe,
no less than the trees and the stars;
you have a right to be here.
And whether or not it is clear to you,
no doubt the universe is unfolding as it should.

Therefore be at peace with God,
whatever you conceive Him to be,
and whatever your labors and aspirations,
in the noisy confusion of life keep peace with your soul.

With all its sham, drudgery, and broken dreams,
it is still a beautiful world.
Be cheerful.
Strive to be happy.

— *Max Ehrmann, 1927*

My Final Thoughts

- Never let the day end without having done something that increases your knowledge, ideas, dreams and goals you wish to obtain.
- Keep moving, learning and implementing new thoughts and insights in your life. Make someone's day.
- Give a compliment, a smile or an encouraging word. Let your time on this earth be a never-ending opportunity to sow seeds of kindness and compassion.
- Live your life with your eyes wide open, your heart unprotected, your mind expanded and your spirit unfettered.

- This is your life to paint, choose bright colors....... feel free to paint outside the lines....it shows uniqueness.
- The suggestions I have given you, will allow you to create the remainder of YOUR life.
- My last and most profound suggestion to you is: Always treat others as you wish to be treated.

Macara Trusty

Macara Trusty has been a leader in the Emergency Medical Services (EMS) career field for over 25 years. She has led and dedicated herself in developing the best EMS provider ensuring they deliver the highest quality of care to the citizens they serve. She is a sought-after speaker sharing her experiences to motivate, inspire and help people grow to their next level. Macara represents her career field well by serving on state and national committees and sits on the Board of Directors for the Hurt & Fallen Foundation. Macara is an individual, and group professional coach, that is helping guide the next generation of leader. She has a Bachelor's Degree in Business, and A Master's Degree in Management and Leadership.

Chapter Twelve

Barriers Become Speed Bumps When You Are Unwilling to Communicate, Collaborate, and Compromise

Advice by Macara Trusty

To understand why I chose this topic for my 25-year-old self, it may help to understand a bit of how I became who I am today. I grew up in a small town. It was one of those towns where everyone knows everyone else, and their business. I was the middle child, with an older brother and younger sister. I was also the "runt" of the family. As a matter of fact, I wore soccer cleats for my kindergarten class picture hoping to NOT be put on the end of the front row because that's where they always put the shortest kids. Wearing the soccer cleats didn't help, by the way. I was also shy, mainly because I was picked on for being one of the shortest kids in the class, so I chose to keep to myself.

I grew up on a cattle ranch and was raised by parents that showed us what it means to work hard for the things you want in life. I was also taught what respect is, what boundaries are, why it's important to follow rules, and to understand "the pecking order" as one of my fathers called it. I was also taught to be independent, fight for what I believed in or was passionate about, and to not be so quick to give up on things that really matter. Those philosophies really began to come together after I was involved in a car accident as a teenager where I broke my back. I went from being a very independent young lady, to a young lady that couldn't take a bath without asking my mother for help. My injury was so severe that I was forced to wear a circumferential back brace that ran the length of my neck to my tailbone. It felt like I was stuck in a hard-plastic barrel. One day I was running across 250 acres of pasture helping herd cattle and the next day I was stuck in a bed having to ask for help in rolling over. There were many times I got very frustrated in having to ask for help. I was angry that I was stuck in that position and that I couldn't do things when I wanted and how I wanted to do them. I would argue with my spinal surgeon on how long I would remain in the hospital after one of my back surgeries and I would negotiate getting to do things like go swimming or walk without my back brace. Although those were tough years in my life, each challenge and the things my parents taught me helped me grow into the young adult I became. They also helped make me a strong and determined female especially while working in a "man's world".

By my senior year, I had overcome so many challenging situations, that I had outgrown my shyness. I had decided I was a force to be reckoned with. I was your average eighteen-year-old high school graduate that was going to not only take on the world, I was going to rule the world! For a while, I really thought I was on the path to do just that, too. The reality was, that was far from being a possibility because I was sabotaging my own career.

Winning with Communication, Collaboration, and Compromise

For a moment, picture in your mind what a bull looks like when you let him loose in a China shop. That was me. I was going to take on the world and change things for the better whether others were on board or not. Shortly after I started my career, I had a clear vision of things that I wanted to see changed and I was on a mission to make that happen whether others agreed or not. I had learned that I could overcome any challenges, especially if I worked hard and followed the rules. I had thought that if I was passionate enough and didn't give up on something, I could accomplish what I wanted. I used the philosophies instilled in me in my youth to help me try to accomplish my goals.

Unfortunately, because I had not yet learned "balance", those philosophies also caused me to struggle in advancing my career or pushing forward projects that I felt very passionate about. There were times where I would want to work on a project, or do something, but someone would disagree. Rather than listen, I would react (sometimes emotionally) and work very diligently to convince them to do it my way or it wouldn't work. If I couldn't convince my superiors to do it my way, I didn't want to participate in it because it would surely fail, and I didn't want to waste my time on a failing project. I worked in a very competitive environment; however, I didn't feel I was competing with my colleagues as much as I wanted to work on projects, I thought would make our organization better. Because I was not in a leadership position, I was regularly accused of "having an agenda". I had to "win". Not only did I have to win the opportunity to work on the project, I wanted to be the one that had the right answer and it had to be done my way. If someone disagreed, or had a different suggestion for my project, I felt I had lost.

Several years later, I was moved into a leadership role within my organization. This position was very political in nature and I learned very quickly that my "bull in the china shop" methods were not going to help me be successful. When attempting to start new projects or enhance current ones, often my passion was mistaken for being argumentative. It doesn't require a PhD to recognize that when others see you as argumentative, often your communication is not as effective, and your audience is not as receptive. If you aren't already aware, it is extremely hard to make organizational changes without support from superiors and colleagues. It is hard to gain support when your superiors and colleagues see you as argumentative and "bullish".

Over time, I learned not only how to pick my battles, but that I really needed to learn the art of compromise. Through my growth in leadership, I came to understand that compromising is not "losing", but through compromise one can accomplish positive change for the greater good. My projects of passion were, in my mind, what I felt was best for the organization. However, without gaining the support of my colleagues, my superiors were less likely to listen, and I was less likely to "win" their support for what I wanted to do.

After several years in various leadership roles, I worked hard daily to practice the art of communication, collaboration, and compromise. While this is an art that requires work every day, I have learned that I am much more successful in accomplishing positive change that expands beyond my department and even beyond my organization.

Communication requires the ability to be authentic and respectful. One doesn't need to try to find the most politically correct verbiage that can take away from the true meaning of the message. Choose your words wisely but choose words that are commonly understood and have a single meaning. As my young adult children say, "stop beating around the bush and get to the point." Sometimes you can gain an ounce of support by simply inviting someone else into the conversation. Many will appreciate that fact that you felt they could provide insight or expertise to what you want to accomplish. To not invite someone that your project will impact can cause colleagues to feel disrespected. Once someone feels they (or their team members in their department) have been disrespected, they "default defensive" and once someone becomes defensive, they are less likely to listen to what you have to say. Remember, if you can't get your colleagues to support your plan, you are less likely to gain support from your superiors as well. It becomes a lose-lose situation for all.

Collaboration is imperative if your project will impact anyone other than yourself. This could include other departments or even other agencies. Depending on what your project involves, it could impact other industries. In my experience, the challenge seems to lie in including all appropriate parties. Often, we fail to recognize who all we should collaborate with. Failure to collaborate could result in frustration, delays, or people becoming "default defensive" and not really engaging in support of the project. Again, if one can't gain support of colleagues, they are less likely to gain support from superiors and it becomes another lose-lose situation. As you are formulating your project outline, it's important to list all departments, or agencies, that might need to be involved each step of the way. It may seem tedious or redundant to do that for every step, but failure to do so could result in missing someone along the way as other agencies may not need to be directly involved until later in the project timeline; however, their input and expertise may be required from the very beginning. Imagine a sprint relay team where the second, third, and fourth members of the team don't play a vital role until later in the race but their participation in the training and preparation is imperative to the success of the team.

Compromise requires the ability to express your goal, with the understanding it may be a shared goal, and agree on steps to reach that goal. This was the most challenging of "arts" for me to learn as it required an understanding that compromising wasn't "losing". It didn't mean that I was giving up on my ideas or giving in. Instead, it was allowing me to gain support for a goal and identify other possible avenues for execution.

Therefore, I would tell my 25-year-old self to take a short-cut. Learn the lessons of communication, collaboration and compromise early on in your career. Being hard-headed, self-justifying and uncompromising tends to keep you from flourishing in the business world. Instead, always be teachable, listen, allow insight and input, and remember when you think you are taking a 'dive' on your ideas you are empowering others to share in a bigger goal!

Debbie Stone

Debbie Stone is an Expert Human Resources Consultant, specializing in Employee Engagement/Satisfaction and organizational process improvement. Her expertise has allowed her the opportunity to develop organizational excellence over vast corporations and assists them in developing into an industry leader. Debbie is a God-Loving woman, who like everyone exceeds to do extraordinary things in her life and in the life of others. She has raised three extraordinary sons, making her exceptional by contributing thoughtful and kind men into the next generation.

CHAPTER THIRTEEN

DREAMS, GONE BY THE WAYSIDE

Advice by Debbie Stone

When I was in high school, it was my DREAM to become a stewardess. I loved to travel. I grew up traveling with my family across the United States. Every year, sometimes in the summer and other times during Christmas, we would drive (or fly) from California to Ohio to visit family. I was very fortunate to see the Grand Canyon, the Rockies, Mt. Rushmore, the painted desert and so many other beautiful places the United States has to offer. I have camped at Yellow Stone National Park, Jelly Stone (oh yeah – Yogi Bear really lives there with Boo-Boo), in the Ruby Marshes of Nevada, rode horses in Utah, I have been so blessed to experience so many historical and magnificent places and things. I have been to every state in the union except one, Alaska (yep, it is on my bucket list – and I will get there one day), and most of them I have visited several times. I have been to several foreign countries that are breathtakingly beautiful. I have the *travel-bug* deep down in my soul, not to mention one heck of an adventurous spirit.

So, like most kids do as they get out of high school, I headed off to college, except it wasn't what I wanted to do. I just wanted to fly in the skies and be free to venture the world. Seeing new places, different people, their culture, the adventure has always captured and peaked my interest (see there I go dreaming again...). As I was sitting in a college class at the very top of the auditorium thumbing through textbooks, as if I were paying attention, I was plotting out a plan to become a stewardess. What was my next move? How do I get there? There must be a way, because I sure have a lot of drive in me. I shechted out a draft in my head and began to put things into motion. I wanted this, and I wanted it bad. I was determined to make it a reality.

I began by calling several different airlines to see what was required of me to obtain an application. See for all you young ins reading this, there were no laptops, no websites, and usually a college or library were the only places you could go to find a desk-top computer. Desk-top computers were the dinosaur-type, big and boxy with a floppy disc (google that to find out what a floppy disc is-Ha Ha). So, in a week or so in my mail box (from the U.S. Postal Service and on my house, no email in-box), I received several applications along with instructions on how to fill it out and where to send it back (yep, you guessed it, via the U.S. Postal Service). But, much to my dismay, there was also a sheet with very specific criteria that you had to meet to even be considered for a job with the airlines as a stewardess. Job criteria in the early 80's was very different than nowadays. A visible tattoo or more than one set of earrings in your ears, just to mention a few, were no-no's (we didn't even know what gage earrings were). There were weight and height requirements. At a minimum you had to be 5 foot 7 inches tall and no more than 135 pounds...hello! Are you kidding me, this 5'2" stature of mine cannot even be 5'7" in heals! And 135 pounds, oh my, well let's just say this girl has curves. Discouraged, but never a broken spirit, I went on to a very different path.

I was basically raised by a single mom (with the exception of her boyfriends or husbands thrown in the mix every now and then) and she did not encouragement or show much leadership to steer me or my brother towards a certain career path when we were growing up. I don't say this as a derogatory dig towards her, but just as a statement because we are generally geared towards our upbringing and so are our parents (unless you can break the cycle). Neither of my parents have a college background or degree, although they were both went on to be very successful in their respective careers. I really didn't even want to be in college, I wanted to take a year off and explore life and work, let's just say I really lacked the ambition to be there.

Fast forward, I "fell" in love halfway through my 1st semester of college and dropped out. I married at 19 and by 20 years of age I had my first son. My dream of becoming a stewardess was gone by the wayside. Life has a way of just 'happening' when you have no real goals or direction. You just live it. Don't get me wrong, I was happy with my life and that boy was my everything. I landed a job in a law firm as a receptionist when I was pregnant with my 1st son and my love for the law was spawn. I switched my 'dream' direction, although I really didn't know much about what that dream was or what it would entail. I will spare you all the ugly details on my way there.

Shortly thereafter I found myself as a single mom and decided I needed to do something more meaningful with my career to be able to support me and my child. I went to Barkley College to obtain my Paralegal Certificate. It was some of the longest days for those 6 months, working 40 hours a week, attending school two nights a week after work, and still being a full-time mommy to a toddler. But I did it and survived. One of the better decisions I have made in my life. After changing jobs a few times to better myself, I stayed within the legal field and I loved what I did. I truly have a passion for the legal system. It has so many different facets. One single word can be interpreted differently. It just never ceases to amaze me. I have worked most of my career in the legal field, as I am always drawn back to it.

Again, LIFE GOES ON (yes the song plays in my head when I say that....'Little Ditty 'bout Jack and Diane' by John Mellencamp. Great song- you can admit it, you were singing it in your head too), I found myself with 3 sons, mid-forty's and thrown back into the workforce. So, I did what I needed to do and found work at an ambulance company (really, I was working 3 jobs for a few years). I was working as their paralegal and shortly hereafter was promoted to their Director of Human Resources. Now, I didn't know what that *title* was, so I had to throw myself in fast and figure it out quick. I was placed in that position because we continued to have one employee lawsuit after another filed against us for various employee violations. We needed to stop the bleeding and I became the tourniquet. We had operations is four states and that gave me just enough opportunity to travel a little bit. My boys were growing up quick and my last one was in high school. This job allowed for the travel bug to be quenched just enough to squash that bug like I stepped on it but didn't quite kill it. There was no splat!

We went through an acquisition in 2011 and I was given more responsibility. I was loving life. I was traveling more, as we were a part of operations that encompassed seven states with the new company. But, like most things in life, every good thing must come to an end (or usually some type of drastic change). In December of 2013, my youngest was in college, the company I was working for abruptly went bankrupt and I found myself lost, absolutely lost and not knowing what to do with myself. My children were grown (for the most part), I was financially not bad off, so I took a few months off to figure it all out.

While I was trying to 'find' myself again, I suddenly realized that the dream I had as a kid was now attainable in this day and age. The days of past where restrictions of height and weight were considered 'sexist' and restraints existed. Where we would just say That-is-Just-How-it-Is! In the 80's it began to slightly change. That was the era where the *Stewardess* name became a *Flight Attendant* due to the term being more gender friendly (there were more men joining the sky's). In the 90's lawsuits were settled regarding specific weight/height restrictions and therefore lifted. The Sky was now in my grasp and I needed to follow my 'teen dream.'

I did It! And OMG it was so scary to pursue that old dream almost 40 years later. I went on a snowy day to Chicago from Ohio to what I call a 'cattle call.' It's when you apply online with an application and then you are either invited or not to the open interview. There are then several steps throughout the day, and you must 'make the cut' to continue on. Last man or woman standing at days end are offered jobs. WooHoo. Winner, Winner, Chicken Dinner, I made it to the end. Ok, so here it comes, the part they don't tell you until the end when they offer you a job:

1. You don't get to choose where you go to train. It is 4-6 weeks long in some remote training facility.
2. You don't get to choose the dates you go to train.
3. You don't get to leave on the weekends during training.
4. You don't get to choose where your home base is.
5. The pay is about $40,000.00 annually.
6. BUT, the perks of flying are pretty awesome.

Some of the above are not so terrible and I could have totally lived with them to fulfill my lifelong dream. Well, put your breaks on. My oldest son was getting married the month they wanted me to train. There was NO bending for them and there was NO bending for me on that one either. Now, I don't regret my decision not to become a flight attendant, because more than anything I finally made my dream come true. I never gave up on it even when it took so many years to come to fruition. Once I obtained it, I found that it wasn't quite what I wanted, but the entire point here, is I never gave up.

So, you see, my 25-year-old self, I have this advise for you....... You are never too old to go back and pick up a dream that you had to let go by the way side to live out life. Sometimes it just takes a little longer to get to there. Timing is powerful. Change can be hard. But to get to some of the really good stuff in your life, you need to be willing to go after dreams, no matter how old they are, no matter how hard they may be to obtain, and no matter if you end up 'getting' them in the end or not. It is that you tried your best to make them happen, and in the end, there may be a different dream that comes out of it that is even better. Go live your life, explore, be an adventure taker, because you never know how long this life will give you. Each day is a beautiful blessing to make dreams happen. Now Self, "WE" have another one to accomplish, let's get to it!

Hhhmmmmm, maybe writing this Chapter, building my self-confidence and putting this out there is one of the things I need to tell you too.......

JENNIFER CORDIA

Jennifer Cordia has been in the healthcare field for over 30 years. She began her career as a candy-striper and worked herself up to the C-Suite leading thousands of healthcare professionals in her career. Her unique style of leadership led to the development of countless Supervisors, Managers Directors, Vice Presidents, and CEO's. Presently, Jennie is the President/CEO of Next Jeneration Logistics training the next "Jeneration" of leaders

Chapter Fourteen

Stay Connected to Your Why & Find Your Brave

Jennifer Cordia's Advice

Older…Certainly. Wiser…. Absolutely.

In the distance a very faint sound of sirens were heard rushing to my aid, I sat very still in the passenger seat of my sister's car as blood poured over my face. The laceration I sustained, from connecting with the windshield as our car crashed into the car ahead, was certainly painful, but mostly just a bloody mess. My lap covered with small shards of glass and my leg pinned under the dashboard that had shifted in an odd manner, almost wrapping itself on us like one of those bars on a rollercoaster. Seatbelts of course, were never discussed and rarely worn and this day was no exception. The noises so individually identifiable; my sister yelling my name, a man trying to open my door asking me over and over to wake up, the blinker clicking on and off, cars breaking swiftly and pulling off to the side of the road as random strangers stopped to help. The distance, consumed with very faint sounds of sirens, coming from many directions that of course grew louder and louder. The unsynchronized cadence of the sirens made them overwhelming and unbearable.

In that very moment of pain and sensory overload, covered in glass and dashboard, unable to open my eyes and having no desire to try, a very pleasant feeling of peace covered me like a blanket. Not sure really if I had passed out or I was dying, I was sure it was the calmest I had ever been. I remember holding onto each moment hoping the feeling would never go away and capturing each second as to never forget pure peace.

That moment, however, did not last long. By this time, what I believed to be 1000 first responders were rocking the car and sticking their hands in my face, while they began yelling different aspects of a plan, aligning the people with tasks, and making comments concerning the need to control the traffic.

The wind began to rush through the windows and the pain from the wound on my head began to increase with such intensity, I attempted to cry out, but just unable to make a noise. A paramedic pushed a hard-plastic mask through the window and began forcing even more air in my face, this, I could not stand at all. The blood now being air-dried, was creating the worst itch I had ever had on the side of my nose and unable to move my arm, I recall feeling that this must be the worst torture I could imagine, an itch you cannot scratch!

The next moment I recall, the room was bright and freezing cold, another 1000 people rushing about removing my cloths and asking me questions, but never waiting for the answers. They were writing on what seemed to be the biggest clip board ever invented. There was a very intense discussion about how no one had a red pen. I was never clear on why red and not blue or black. I am not sure what part of the process necessitated a red pen; however, I was very sure that the lack of a red pen was creating frustration and distraction. One nurse stated she went to the office supply store to buy a bag of red pens, and yet she still cannot find one. Many of the nurses were shuffling about discussing how the drug reps never bring red pens how helpful it would be if they did. They were opening and closing drawers looking for a red pen. Alas! a red pen! I heard loudly from across the room, loud sighs of relief and then

#!^%$##, the red was dried out. Again, the staff could be heard ranting over the critical pen dilemma.

All the sudden, shivering and all alone, strapped down to a hard wood board with my neck in a brace that was cutting off my air, and with blood pooled into both of my eyes, the itch still looming, pain in many different spots as I was rapidly being stuck and poked and pulled and pushed, a warm hand grabbed mine. I remember so clearly the way the way the warm washcloth soaked on my face and cleaned the blood from my eyes, allowing me for the first time to open them.

I saw a beautiful woman peering at me, her face seemed as big as the room. She stated, "My name is Barb, I am here, I have always been here, I will always be here with you and everything is going to be fine". I then fell fast asleep as with those words, a sense of absolute safety rushed over, I just sank into the hard wood board I was lying on and honestly the itch was insignificant.

I knew at that moment my life would change and I was certain that I would spend the rest of it serving those in need, caring for sick and injured, and making a difference in the lives of those who were scared and vulnerable.

My career in healthcare has now spanned 30 years and I have embraced every role, every moment and every adventure.

I as reflect on my path, at 25 years old my journey was just starting to unfold. I was active as an Emergency Department Nurse. I had achieved my goal and I was an Emergency Department registered nurses. I believed I was excelling in this role and loved each moment. I was now the nurse in every trauma room, caring for as many patients as possible and ensuring that I imparted that same feeling of comfort and safety I had been afforded so many years ago.

I was *THE* face; I had actually become the face that I had remembered. I was the nurse who was peering into the eyes of those who were scared or in pain (believing of course I was just as beautiful as Barb) and it was now my hands that embraced so many others as I conveyed care and caring, and trust and safety.

The drive I possessed to care for patients and their families became very clearly what fueled me each day and was what certainly "filled my bucket." I was almost frantic to learn more and mentor more, to teach more and research more. I knew that I needed to take every opportunity to become a significant force in healthcare.

My fortune was incredible, as I had experienced such an event in my past that exposed the passion I was harboring to heal and comfort and protect in a way that many do not encounter. The experience of being a young trauma patient was the pinnacle of my career, as that is where it began.

That fortune, that feeling of excitement and connection and passion and caring are what allowed me to be the best and to model excellence. It is this very passion, this connection that I would tell my younger self to embrace.

My advice to my 25 year old self is to lead always with passion, with a palpable connection to that passion in ***every*** moment, in ***every*** opportunity and in ***every*** challenge, and ***never*** forget or disconnect from the moments and the people and the events that illuminated my path to begin with.

Looking back, I do believe that for a very long time my journey every day began with that connection to my "why". I was always the leader who working side by side in every department with those providing care. I demanded that every co-worker was treated with respect, their voices were heard and their environment complete with everything they needed to care for the patients who presented and trusted us with their lives. They would always have a red pen. I continued along my path in the exact same manner, whether those who were entrusted to me numbered 20 or 2000.

While demanding excellence, I also modeled excellence, and my boots were always on the very same ground.

Embarrassed to admit in such a forum, I can recall moments of time and portions of my past where I was not connected, where I did not lead with the passion inside me, where I failed.

As I recollect the past, I have great clarity on the times in my career where I did allow myself to disconnect. Completely aware of what I "should" have done, and now wiser to the world and to myself, to the art and science of leadership, I see where I made decisions to not engage, where my instincts were dismissed or excused away and I was simply moving by and never stepping in.

I often wonder if those moments were the very moments that created limitations to my journey. I am certain they were moments that tainted it for sure.

Examining these times has been a very interesting exercise for me and I do wish that I had some of those moments to "re-due". I believe there are 4 factors that are at the forefront of challenges I have faced. These factors will support you as you make a decision that is not consistent with your history, that does not reflect the reputation you have created and causes you to forget your "why".

The first factor, and perhaps the most difficult to recognize is the skillful use of excuses. This space of emptiness carries a void that is lonely and confusing, and I now understand, is fueled only by the excuse that is created.

Excuses are the reason you provide, to yourself or to others why you are not performing to the standard you would expect.

There are many excuses that are logical, and many times they are quickly validated by others. The ability to adopt the excuse does depend on the character, experience and relationship of those who the excuse are being created. Explaining that the two children you have require so much attention, attending a staff meeting is impossible, to a single mom of 7 children who is always present at every staff meeting, will not be the path you want to take as this mom will struggle to empathize.

An excuse for one person is not an excuse for another. Beliefs and individual core focus vary as do our expectations of ourselves.

The second factor I have found is fear, or what I would state as the inability to find "your brave". The ability to be brave is not a trait examined often by leaders, however the ability to push past the fear is admirable and allows the passion to direct the success.

One such moment I recall occurred during the first year of my very first management position. I was asked by leaders in the organization to take on the responsibility of managing the Emergency Department with 130 employees and a renovation looming. I had no real leadership experience but was very excited and very interested to learn all I could. I was a very strong clinician and spent hours each night learning all I could about ED medicine and how to improve the care. I was active in ENA (Emergency Nurse Association), and I was certified in everything I could find. I also instructed courses and took every opportunity I could to teach nursing students as well as nurses young and old.

I was sitting at my desk and received a call from the national headquarters of ENA. They were asking me if I would have interest in chairing a committee focused on trauma care. I was literally frozen in my chair. I remember thinking "why they would call me"? Why would they take that time to search me out and ask me to be accountable for such an enormous task? I did quickly take a deep breath and immediately said "no".

My heart was telling me to jump on the opportunity to chair a committee at the national level on a topic I was extremely passionate about, but I truly believed I was excellent at. I was overwhelmed with fear of looking un-educated. I did not hold an MSN as many others did, and I was petrified to look silly. Certainly, I was intellectually aware that my strength was in this area of Emergency Medicine and I was very comfortable in my immediate surroundings being the sought-after resource, however fearful the complement of my knowledge would not be enough for national scrutiny. I wanted desperately to be a part of the team and to have an opportunity to chair, and frozen with the idea of doing it. This was my chance to break into a national forum, and I did not take it because I was afraid.

Of course, someone did accept the offer, and I followed that leader as she chaired the committee with grace and confidence. She used the opportunity to publish and speak in many different venues on the great work accomplished. Her career blossomed and her position solidified in ENA. This was a moment in my past, I am certain had I made the choice to lead with passion and not fear the outcome would have most certainly been a success.

I believe the third factor is simply the danger of assumptions. This factor is the one that has had the greatest negative impact on my career. I have assumed, the direction of an outcome, the opinions and thoughts of others, even the strategic direction of executive leaders and hospital systems. I have been incorrect many times and disappointed often as the outcome is not successful. I did however continue this behavior and truly, somehow, I was still amazed at the negative results.

I have learned that the assumption, the story I create is coming only from my vantage point. I make these assumptions based on *my* beliefs and from *my* mindset and that of course is not the mindset of everyone. I have had moments in my career that I have decided to walk one way or the other and have chosen a path inconsistent from an intellectual perspective as well as ignoring that feeling in my gut.

During a very critical time in my career I managed to make a very clear decision, based on an enormous assumption that would lead to my very own demise.

I had been selected to be part of a team selecting a new leader. This was a task I was honored to be selected for and intended to be successful in the candidate chosen. Aware this decision was critical to thousands of patients, families, co-workers, and the community. I assumed the responsibility with great conviction and determination. The candidate was chosen. To ensure success, I *assumed* the best direction for me to proceed was to ensure successful onboarding and assimilation of the candidate into the role.

The decision I made was to set aside my personal goals and development plans for one year and support the new leader. I planned serve as a resource, and ensure the candidate was afforded every opportunity to be successful. I was very well intended and *assumed* the other party would welcome the support, and assistance. I quickly realized that the decision I had made was an error. I had assumed the direction my passion and always led me would align with the new leader I had decided to "hitch my wagon to". I assumed my core dedicated to servant leadership would be similar to the candidate and together we would accomplish great things. I now see I was blinded by my assumptions and in that same moment my beliefs and core values sitting at the core of what drives my passion were being suffocated. The reality was the candidate and I were nothing alike. I feared now for the community and the patients and the co-workers. This partnership would not end well, and had I validated my initial assumptions thus making them facts, I would have not chosen to put my goals aside.

Assumptions are always just that, an assumption. All assumptions are not wrong, but they are at best a great guess. My advice – Do not assume!

The fourth factor is the one that is the most difficult to identify, the most difficult to admit, and the most detrimental to you career, and the easiest to repair. The Emotional Drift from your Passion (EDP), is certainly a factor that plagues leaders of all tenure, all levels, all genders and all organizations. EDP is not limited to leaders and can be apparent as people are serving in any role, from volunteers to CEO's.

There is a bit of similarity between EDP and what is commonly referred to as "burnout" however burnout has many additional layers and very often is more difficult to effect and reverse.

I remember the first moment I started to realize this was an issue. I was sitting at my desk during a typical morning for sure. Quite voices saying hello in the hallway, the faint smell of coffee brewing and the sun peeking through the dreadful drapes in my office. I began to gather my work for the day. I had my note pad for taking endless notes in endless meetings, my calendar of where to be and when, my phone of course to allow notification of the errors and issues of the day, and my cup for coffee to help me get through it. I began to hear faintly in the distance sirens in the distance. The sirens were one and then another and then another. They were becoming louder and louder and the cadence was so off it became overwhelming a bit. I walked over to horrible heavy tapestry drapes to see fire trucks and police cars, ambulances and support vehicles screech into the ambulance bay. I looked back at the phone that was sitting on my desk and instead of grabbing it and running straight down to the Emergency Department as I had done hundreds of times before I continued to look at it, I let the drapes fall back and sat back down. I was telling myself that they did not need me and the staff that was working in the ED would handle the situation.

As I sat in my chair it was so foreign to me as I distinctly remember feeling nothing. I did not feel emotion for the patients who were suffering from the incident, the staff who may be stressed, the first responders who were tired and exhausted or the other patients and families who would need to wait as the care of the trauma patients would come first. I had let my crown fall to the floor.

EDP is dangerous when the role you are serving no longer emits emotion. Each day, each moment the role we choose to serve in should always emit emotion from our "gut". As leaders we should be emotional regarding work we do, the people we lead, the colleagues we partner with and the outcomes we elicit.

One of the most important points to remember when dealing with EDP is that work should always be emotional, however it should never be personal. I have witnessed over the years many people who continue to make work personal and the reality is work is business, work is work. It must always be emotional; it should never become personal.

The formula is very simple. People are successful when they find something, they are passionate about, they remember the "why", they remember the tragedy from which greatness grew. That passion, that why, that tragedy must be worn proudly and displayed always and revered constantly like a fantastic crown of jewels.

As we go through our journey each day, we encounter disappointment, we are faced with mindless complaining from adults for ridiculous reasons, we are passed up for promotions, we miss our families desperately, we are surveyed endlessly, we are always on call and we never have a solid night sleep. Depending on our role we begin to become physically separated from where our journey began. This separation occurs with walls in or offices to the meetings rooms that consume most of the day, to the travel that sends us miles apart, or the paperwork that becomes so overwhelming there is no time left. With each of these inevitable intrusions it is possible that barriers begin form between you and your crown. Each jewel becoming faded and old and soon the crown becomes so heavy with burden you simply let it drop to ground. Work continues and you are moving through each day, however not even for a moment are you truly a part of any day.

This is when you are no longer emotional, you are no longer able to truly feel the work you once loved.

EDP is easy to rectify. Admitting this has occurred is truly the first step. Admitting that you are separated from the work you once loved is not an easy task but is critical in moving past it. It is very easy to reconnect with your "why", you simply must return to where you first discovered your passion. Then you must engulf yourself in very similar moments and the rush of emotion will return. I have referred to this moment as "finding my Jesus" and believe it perfectly reflects the event.

So, to you my 25-year-old self:

My advice to you is to stay connected to your "why", never stop spending time in the very place you discovered your passion, never make assumptions, find your brave, and ensure that there is always a red pen.

Chapter Fifteen

My Family, Friends and Peers Advice to You

My friend and mentor John Maxwell has a great quote, "if it is lonely at the top, you are not doing something right". As a practice, I have always tried to share my opportunities and successes with my family, friends and peers. This project is no exception. I sent out to all that know me the invitation to share their advice to their 25-year-old self and this is what they came up with.

If you are not where you want to be right now, remember there is plenty of time to get there, enjoy the journey. ***Robin Blanchard***

Keep your pride and your ego in check; when you think you've done that, check it again. Back in the early days, being on the ambulance as this industry was gaining prominence was really heady stuff, and the results of that hubris could be dangerous. Battle lines were drawn with nurses, firefighters and just about everyone else who was not "us." As damaging as those relationship issues were, "ego" on an ambulance can be fatal. "We all have calls we're not done running," Janet Smith of On Assignment has said to me during some long, soul-searching conversations. The call that flows through my consciousness to this day — when I am in that state between dreaming and waking — happened while I was a First Aid cardholder working as an ambulance attendant in a rural Calif. town in 1975.

I was six months into this part-time job (called to the station by pager for $5 a call), and at 22 years old, I was pretty sure I knew just about everything I needed to know about running ambulance calls. After all, I certainly knew how to recognize a drunk when I saw one. One afternoon, we responded to a wreck that didn't seem that bad and transported a man who reeked of alcohol non-emergency due to his "back pain." He was acting irrational, thrashing about so much I really couldn't get a good set of vitals, because, after all, he was drunk, right? We arrived at the emergency room, and when we passed the front entrance, the ER doc sitting at the desk reached over to the rotary phone and called in surgery — STAT. The patient died in the elevator. When I realized what had happened, I was sure I killed him, so I quit the squad.

The doctor — God bless him — called me at home and had me come to the ER. He sat me down and convinced me that if the accident had happened in front of the hospital, he couldn't have saved this man with his massive internal injuries. But he did tell me this: "Learn from this. On any call, irrational behavior is hypoxia until proven otherwise." If rookie me had heard that earlier, it would have saved me a lot of pain.... **Steven L. Athey**

Worrying about promotions and accolades at 25 are less important than building strong family and friend relationships. Be humble, and care more about others than yourself. Employers come and go but meaningful relationships may be lost forever. Take good care of your wellbeing and mental health. **Eric Graham Chase**

Listen more and talk less, you don't know shit kid! **Ruben Farnsworth**

The best advice I could give my 25-year-old self would be to work at and master a skill that makes you want to teach someone else who feels the same passion that you do. Those people will find you. Those people will help you. Those people will teach you. If you do not have passion for something, then you just have a job. With passion and commitment, you have purpose and a career ahead. **Dave Nestor**

Pursue your dreams and figure out your goals and then learn how to achieve them. * Let go of the past feelings, they will not define you in the long run. * Re-chart your course if necessary. * Spend time with the people who bring out the best in you and spend less time with those who stir the worst traits.* Last but not least, instead of looking for a hook up, or someone to date for a while, wait for that one special person you can spend the rest of your life with. You got this! **Bill Meyer**

Listen to your gut more, and the world less. **Kaye Sheets**

Don't be too stubborn to ask for help. At 25 years old I had to work a cardiac arrest on my dad. I was unable to save him and took my feelings and suppressed them so deep, it caused me to become an emotional rock. My marriage suffers at times even today because of it. The Post Traumatic Stress it caused me eventually became an issue over the course of my career. **Bobby Fields**

The future years are going to be coming and fast. Do not wait to get started, the best time to begin is right now. **Zachery R. Cebollero** – (Author note: This is my son, I am very proud of my boy, but he should have added, *listen to your Dad more* – Chris Cebollero)

Stay focused and complete your college degree. Does not matter if it is an Associates, Bachelors or higher. Just stay the course and get it done. **Jon Dahlvig**

Listen to the people that love you. I would have been in a sales career far earlier and not married my first husband had I listened and realized those around me were seeing what I could not. * Pay cash for everything, credit cards are the devil. * Save 10% of your take home check and max out your 401k every month. * Do not quit a job without having another one. * Do not worry about finding the "one" you will find that person at the right time. * You have to learn to love yourself and being by yourself before you can truly love another person. * Live your life every day, life may seem long at 25, but it goes by so quickly. * Live without regrets, to do that try everything you want to. * If you are considering something for yourself, ask yourself this question, "is what I am about to do, will I regret tomorrow"? Sometimes you may regret it, but find the reflect on that situation, learn from it and gain that needed wisdom. It is not worth beating yourself up over failure or mistakes. * Do not look in the past and try to return to it. If you have walked away from something or someone, there was a good reason, it is a big windshield, and a small rearview mirror for a reason. * Everything happens for a reason, never beat yourself up over mistakes or failures, everyone will be making mistakes in their life you are no different, the secret is learning from them. First time you do something wrong it is a mistake, second time it is a choice. * Find a career that is all about something you love to do, work is easy to do every day if you are going to be happy doing it. * Trust your gut feelings, if there is an ounce of doubt listen to it. There is a good reason that you are feeling what you are. This is the basis of developing your intuition * Have faith in yourself, sometimes it doesn't feel like it at 25, but you can achieve ANYTHING you put your mind to. Keep trying and never give up. You have everything to gain and nothing to lose. * Learn to love some kind of exercise whether it's playing on a team or time in the gym, your body will thank you later. * Learn to cook and eat healthy, developing that skill early will take care of you your whole life. * Take mental health days if you need it, there is nothing wrong with taking care of yourself, and if you need help there is no shame in getting it. * Be there for your best friends and if someone isn't there for you in a time of need, and if this is consistent, they aren't real friends. * Always stay true to your heart and values. * If you aren't treated like a queen, move on. * Never ever let someone tear you down, know you are worthy and respect yourself enough to not let anyone treat you differently. * Last but not least, buy the best mattress you can, sleep is critical and good sleep is priceless. **Liz Roberts**

Chris Cebollero told me one time; *"it is okay to be greener than a leprechaun's ass. Embrace what you don't know and learn from it"*. You are surrounded by mentors that will shape your career and build your foundation for being a leader later. Do not take these people for granted. You will not have this opportunity as wholesome as it is now. Slow down your mind and activities and take in what is being said. Hear twice as much as you speak. Work with the hard asses, they will mold you. Do not turn away from hard shifts, partners or times. Put in and pay your dues, and always earn your keep. Nothing is handed to you and what is handed to you is not worth keeping. **Jessie Wallace**

No one can do it alone. **Rick Bazan**

You are worthy as you are. You will not be able to change her and compromising who you are for her will not end well. Read the red flags for what they are and RUN! **Matthew Kauffmann**

Do not be afraid to listen to experience. **Jeri Smith**

Dear 25-year old dumb girl Stop it!! Stop looking for worth in all the wrong places. Stop trying to walk in a purpose that isn't yours!! * Slow down and listen, you don't have to be everything to everyone, nor a door mat for those that do nothing but use you!! * Good God woman, know and respect your worth, and don't forget to add the tax! * Stop giving people discounts and rent head space that haven't earned it. * Live the skin you're in. * Be kind even if it hurts. * Walking away isn't quitting, you are beautiful just the way you are to the right person. * Know sweet darling, it gets so much better. * There will be all kinds of wonderful and heart ache, and it is worth every single moment. **Melanie Barrett**

This isn't looking back far for me, only 2 years, but I had an interesting year when I was 25, lost my father and made the decision to go to medical school and I think my personality has changed a lot in only 2 years. That being said my advice to myself is - there's only a finite amount of time in life and when an opportunity presents itself, take it because it may lead to new opportunities and take you to places you didn't even imagine. **Tom Latosek**

What you deem as success at 25 is not what you will define it as later...relationships are the key to success. The relationship with yourself, family, friends, coworkers and those who enter and leave your life for brief or long periods. See the gift in those relationships and be grateful- it is your choice every day to be happy. **Holly Stewart**

Simple . . . It's going to be ok! **Debbie Self**

Don't expect perfection of yourself because you only set yourself up for failure that way. Allow yourself to make mistakes and learn. Sometimes we learn our best lessons from our mistakes. Yes, we try our best always but don't beat yourself up when you make a mistake. Know your worth and don't allow anyone to disrespect you or use your mistakes and self-doubt to manipulate you into things that aren't really you. ***Christy Pieren***

Look back on how you were raised, what your parents taught you, showed you, explained to you. Ask yourself what was it all for? What did it all mean? Those were the years that were molding me for my future and I never knew that! I wish I would have thanked them a million times over for the mentoring they gave me to guide me on my path to a successful career. ***Joyce Brown***

Every conversation should include three of the following words: please, thank you, sir, and ma'am. * Treat every patient like how you'd want your grandmother to be treated. * They're mad at the uniform, not you. They don't even know you, so don't take stuff personally. * You'll like this job much better when you finish your bachelor's degree and you don't HAVE to do it. * Your boss is probably not an idiot when he tells you to do something stupid. He has to deal with his boss and his bosses boss telling him to do stupid. * People are nice and usually do the right thing, except when they don't. * Have pride in doing your job-don't let the other first responders carry your equipment, carry your patients, etc. We provide the medical care, cops solve crimes, firefighters fight fires. * EMS, at least in Manhattan, is as much about eating at great ethnic restaurants and seeing the backstage of everything as it is about doing jobs. Take advantage of the first two everyday while owning your area. You're going to see some pretty cool stuff! * This isn't so much for the young me as for a lot of other folks (I was fortunate to be making $75k on the 1990s as a street medic)-you deserve to be paid a fair living wage salary with decent benefits for your work. Don't let anybody tell the money isn't there, it is. Fight for it. * Max out that 401k, you idiot. ***Scot Phelps***

Be kind to self and others, honest, because Karma will show up. Also, blood is not always thicker than water...Sometimes friends will love and accept you more. **Nena Lee**

If you're not saving $ in your 401K or equivalent for YOUR future now, start ASAP! **Brian Brelje**

"Dear 25-year-old self, what held me back the most was the lack of self-confidence and social anxiety. For a slightly quicker, less painful, and more meaningful trajectory to your most authentic self, I recommend the following. First, duct tape the mouth of your inner critic. Put more energy into changing the way you see yourself than how you think others might see you. Second, find a mentor. Mentors will save your bacon, become your lifelong friends and be your greatest allies. Work hard, reach your goals then reach back and become a mentor to someone else. Last, be afraid but let courage push you through fear. Do the scary thing anyway. Regret has a greater penance than fear." **Catie Holstein**

It's ok to fail at times. That's how you grow and learn. That you don't have to be the best at everything, as long as **you're the best** version of yourself. **Jennifer Dones**

Don't work yourself to death to make a buck. Enjoy life!!! **Bec O' Bar**

When I was 18 years old, I got a full-time job at Maspeth Federal Savings. This was our local bank that was a big part of our community. Over the next 18 years, I advanced in titles but basically supervised our drive thru night shift. I loved working the hours from 12:15 to 8:15 pm as I got to know the people I worked with and loved the all. I have always been an imaginative person, in what of course was the most unimaginative job ever. Wanting to use my creative skills, I joined the uniform committee,

I became their first Archivist, was part of their anniversary event, and helped organize and shop for the yearly Children's Christmas Party. As a practice, I would decorate people's offices for their life's events, and much more. A friend of mine, many years earlier, said that shed visit and in 30 years from now I would still be in the same job. To be honest, that comment scared the hell out of me. Low and behold, my partner, now my husband, got a job at the new Nordstrom that was opening on Long Island. I was happy for him and watch how fast he was promoted in his new division. It inspired me to get a part time job. This was really a get opportunity for me, and I came to life in this part time role, and I became a new person. The opportunity arose with Nordstrom to move to Scottsdale, Chicago, Portland than Seattle. I met amazing people, celebrities and made lifelong friends. It was an amazing ride. So, the moral of this story and the advice I'd give to my 25-year-old self would be, don't settle for a safe boring job that does not fulfill **ALL** of you. Find the one that redevelops you into the person you are destined to be. **Chris Giusto**

Take time to truly appreciate your self-worth and abilities. * Know that pain as horrible as it is will ease over time. * Learn from life lessons and you will never make a mistake. * Accept your flaws and they will become your strengths. * Learn what happiness is and this it is not defined by another person but defined by your true inner self. * Finally, buy 2 shares of Berkshire Hathaway. ***Jay Cebollero***

You will be inclined to take this journey all on your own- you *could* do it, but you will cover more ground and progress faster if you have a team. Find people you trust that care about you. You will know them when you find them; they're the ones you feel like yourself with, that's your "tribe." It's not necessary that you all have the same goals- but that you have goals and help each other with them and support each other on the trip.

You will also need a guide. A mentor. No, you don't know everything- someone else having a map already will help you navigate what you don't know. This is another relationship where trust and mutual respect is key. I wandered about for 17 years before I found these people and hit the fast track. Don't get bogged down in your ego and allow people to help you, your contributions to society and industry depend on it. **Amy Eisenhauer**

Authors Note: *We all have that one friend; we know them well. The one that makes you shake your head, the one you do not put on speaker phone, and the one that makes you smile when your day sucks. Ladies and Gentlemen, this is that one friend for me. Chris Cebollero*

Don't sweat he petty things, just pet the sweaty things. Rub some dirt on it and harden up. All bleeding stops eventually. Sliding a pencil up your butt if you are constipated works better than laxatives. **Tim Quandt**

Note:

Note: